Family Spirituality for Busy People

Irene Marinelli

Our Sunday Visitor Publishing Division
Our Sunday Visitor, Inc.
Huntington, Indiana 46750

ISBN: 0-87973-149-4
Cover design by James McIlrath
149

Thanks to my husband Robert and to my children, Rob, Beth, Jay, Noelle and Christopher, who shared it all with me, then stayed out of my way so I could write it down.

The Family is, so to speak, the domestic Church. In it parents should, by their word and example, be the first preachers of the faith to their children. -Lumen Gentium, 11

Table of Contents

Introduction

This book is a practical guide for families who want to build traditions of family prayer, family faith rituals and family Bible reading. Many books offer valuable information on these subjects, but I have yet to find one that gives a play-by-play description of *how* to begin praying or reading the Bible in the middle of a busy life with a houseful of children. This book proposes to do just that. It can be done. We have done it, and I hope you will find within these pages a guide that will make it not only possible for you, but easier than you ever imagined.

Questions and more questions

As you begin to explore this exciting new goal for your family, so many questions will surface and keep surfacing. How do I ease my family into a regular prayer time? At what age should I begin to read the Bible to my children? What about teenagers, will they not resent this intrusion into their time?

As we deal with these questions, you will be able to see possibilities for change and growth that will seem feasible. We are relying on experience, not someone's vague idea of how an ideal family should react, but the struggles of a real family (one far from ideal) to come to terms with these challenges and meet the goals of spiritual unity.

Getting Started

Take one tired parent at the end of the day, add a reluctant uncomfortable spouse and several resistent, foot-dragging children. Mix together for an hour or so with a snatch of Bible reading, a smattering of prayer and you have a mess, a mutiny, an ultimate failure. Nobody makes much sense of it and you, the one who pried them all away from their favorite television program, are left with a sense of total failure and frustration.

I cannot tell you how often this scene was enacted at our house. Finally I sat down one day and admitted that we were getting nowhere and asked myself why. Why were my children and my husband so turned off? Why was all my hard work creating chaos instead of unity? I knew that family prayer, Scripture reading and home rituals were important enough to become a part of our family routine. Why were my

6

attempts so unsuccessful?

Up to that point I had been orchestrating everything in a nicely organized way with neat little readings and packaged rituals and prayers. I had arbitrarily decided, after reading several books on the subject, that beginning immediately, we were going to pray together and read Scripture together and say grace and bedtime prayers and create home rituals for all the big holidays. There was no end to my enthusiasm. It all sounded so good when I had read the books. Those book children — how they all cooperated! And the husbands — they gratefully cleared dinner dishes and switched off football games in their zealous efforts to contribute.

It should have been obvious to anyone that there was a wide chasm between a mythical "book family" and a living, breathing, I-want-my-own-way family. Time, effort and lots of trial and error lay between reading a book on home liturgies and actualizing that book into a living tradition in a real family. The pitfalls are many and the *immediate* rewards are few.

I had plunged into this without much preparation, without prayer and, worst of all, without the support of my family. Why weren't they supportive, these dear ones of mine? They had no idea what I was trying to accomplish. I did not tell them. It was my ball, and they had to play the game my way. I had forged ahead with beginner's enthusiasm without being wary of the pitfalls. In this book we will review the pitfalls while keeping a vision of the ideal.

This book was written between diaper changing and cookie baking. We began our home rituals when we had three children. Now we have five. During the intervening years we have changed jobs, homes, cities, and careers. Through it all our commitment to the spiritual growth of our family has not changed. This book is about process, not content. We are concerned here with exploring the method that best suits your particular family situation, your special people and your home.

The biggest question is, of course, how to get it all rolling, how to make the plunge and stay afloat. Are you about to jump into this in the middle of a growing family and an unsuspecting spouse? First of all, your spouse need not — must not — be unsuspecting. As in all other aspects of the family's spiritual life, find time to talk to your spouse about desire for these new traditions and try to enlist his or her cooperation, enthusiasm and active participation, if possible. Choose a time when you can talk privately and state your feelings as honestly as possible. A righteous pose has no place here. As one concerned adult to another, discuss your ideas and any objections your spouse might have. A spouse's reaction to what you are proposing can vary from glad exclamations that you have discovered these new and important expressions of family spirituality, to a dark and stubborn rejection of anything religious or "churchy."

People vary in their approach to God, to faith, to prayer. My husband fell somewhere in the middle. He did not embrace me with tears of joy, but he did not oppose my suggestions either. He logically pointed out some very real problems that lay in the way of our home rituals, and we were able to work those out — together.

What if your spouse refuses to have anything to do with prayer, rituals or Scripture reading family style? The Apostle Peter points to a clear path in these matters. He says: "Wives, in the same way be submissive to your husbands so that if any of them do not believe the Word, they may be won over without talk by the behavior of their wives, when they see the purity and reverence of your lives" (1 Peter 3: 1-2).

Admitting that the word "submissive" has little place in modern vocabulary, let us look at this passage from a different angle. If we interpret "be submissive" to mean be respectful, and we consider the words "without talk" to mean without nagging, the passage makes complete sense. State your piece. Let your partner know how important this is to you and to the family. Then, that is it. No nagging. No punishing. No pouting.

Peter goes on to say, "Always be prepared to give an answer to everyone who asks you to give the reason for the hope that you have. But do this with gentleness and respect" (1 Peter 3: 15-16). Again Peter's message: respect. Underline it in your mind. Never, no matter what, push your spouse into a corner, especially in front of the children. Keep these initial discussions private: no children, no in-laws, no outsiders. Only after things are settled between the two of you should you include the other people who live in your house. If any of them are above the age of six, the discussions will be lively, I promise you.

If after you have prayed and talked to your spouse and prayed some more, he or she still refuses to have anything to do with this new venture, what then? You could gather your courage and go ahead alone. You might simply inform your partner that you have decided to begin and you would like some cooperation, even if that cooperation only extends to benevolent silence. I stress the word "benevolent." It does you no good to have a thundercloud face across the table as you attempt to say grace or read Scripture with the children before meals. If you cannot convince your spouse to join in with the family, perhaps he or she would be willing to be a passive observer. Take comfort in the fact that you do not have to deal with a boisterous opposition.

The presence of both parents at these rituals will do much to underline their importance to your children if and only if that presence is gracious and accepting. If sharing these home liturgies with the family makes a husband or wife so uncomfortable that a dark cloud is cast over the whole thing, it would be better for all concerned if the dissenting partner just stayed away for a time. When the routines are established and home rituals become firmly fixed traditions in your home, you might ask your spouse to join you. The disapproval at this point will not cause nearly the confusion and mutiny it would have at the beginning.

Suppose your spouse, instead of just backing away from the ideas you present, totally refuses to *allow* home rituals, Scripture reading and prayer in the house. He or she has let you know in fiery terms that "This is my house!" and "churchy nonsense" is off-limits here. He or she may even throw in the fact that "I am earning money for the family, and I make the rules."

Is it his or her house exclusively? Have you led your partner to believe that over the years? Are your rules shared? Obviously, you *both* work hard to keep the family going. You *both* love your children. Before you label your spouse a lost cause and the most stubborn person alive, jump over to the other side of the fence for a minute. Perhaps sometime in his or her past there may have been an experience related to religion that brought about deep hurt, wounds that only scarred over and did not completely heal. None of us can ever know another's relationship with God, not really, not in the deepest sense.

You have two choices here. You can drop the whole thing or you can pray and talk with your minister or priest and then make a decision. Whatever you decide in the end, consider all the people who live in your house, not just the other adult. Your decision will not be an easy one, and I cannot advise you beyond what I have said already: talk with your minister or priest. Pray. Talk lovingly with your spouse. Then ... decide. If your decision involves going ahead with the home rituals, you may be in for some real problems. Be honest. If your home is run by a man or woman who will not give an inch to those who live there, especially to the marriage partner, you already have significant problems. The issue of home rituals did not bring about these problems. It may have brought them out into the open — all the better for you to face and deal with, all the better to heal.

Suppose you are the head of a single parent family. For the time being you are obliged to be both father and mother to your children. You probably hold down a full-time job. Perhaps you are taking some evening courses to advance your position and fatten your pay check. You may be struggling to come to terms with visitation rights, solitary evenings or the startling realization that the responsibility for these young lives under your roof is yours alone. There never seems to be enough money coming in, and the lonely hours after the children's bedtime are still difficult for you.

Now you want to add to all this a new ritual of family prayer and Bible reading. Certainly your problems are numerous but one of the concerns you *do not* have is convincing a reluctant spouse that these family traditions are enriching and important. Since you alone are the head of your household now, you need answer to no one for your decision.

On the other hand, it might be nice to have another adult to share these new rituals with you, especially if your children are very young. Having another adult to help with the planning, to keep schedules on track until the traditions take root may be encouraging for you as well as your children. Again, look around. See what you have to work with. How can you use what you already have in your life to full advantage?

If you happen to live close to your extended family, start there. You may have brothers or sisters with children not too far removed in age from yours. Would it be feasible to bring the whole cousinly clan together for some prayer time? Scripture reading? Perhaps some special holiday rituals?

If you live in close proximity to your grown siblings, you are probably aware of their attitudes about religious traditions and home rituals. However, tread softly here. You and your brother may be on the same wave length when it comes to taxes, consumer issues, political views. Religion could be another matter altogether. Just because you both may attend the same church does not guarantee that you look at your faith in the same way. If your sibling recoils at the mere suggestion of pooling your collective children for some home prayers and rituals, stop right there and look elsewhere for a partner.

If your extended family yields no fertile soil consider a friend, preferably a friend whose situation approximates yours. It is best to team up with someone who has no spouse to consider and consult. Once in a great while it happens that your relationship with both partners in a friend's marriage is equally warm and congenial. If this is the case, and you feel that this couple may be open to teaming up with your family to bring new traditions of spirituality to both your homes, by all means give it a try.

You might approach your priest or minister and find out if there are single parents in your parish who would be open to discussing the type of home rituals and prayers you have in mind.

One precaution here: while it is good to have two on the adult

11

team, be careful not to leap too quickly. Remember you are working toward the development of an ongoing tradition for your family. Get to know the person you will be partnering with before jumping right in with prayer time or Bible time or other rituals. It might be a good idea to get all the children together several times at a picnic or some backyard play at your house. Often adults assume that all like-age children are compatible. Nothing could be further from reality! Nor should you assume that friendship will blossom between all thirty-five-year olds. Go slowly at first. You do not want to have to back off after a few prayers or Bible reading sessions because *now* you see with perfect clarity that you have made a disastrous choice.

A single friend whom you know, love and trust is the best partner for the project you have in mind. The ideal situation of course, would be for your children and your friend's children to be close in age and friendly with each other.

Going ahead

Now, let us assume that you have had a quiet, low-keyed talk with your spouse or adult friend. He or she understands and is willing to help. Your house is filled with several small children, perhaps a baby and at least one pre-teen or adolescent. The children's friends come and go. After school activities are numerous and relatives drop in now and again. You are always involved in a struggle with time and money and snatching minutes here and there for your own thoughts, your own privacy. This is the situation most families find themselves in. Now you come to drop this new idea squarely in their midst. How will they react? How will you cope?

Unlike dealing with the other adult who shares your life, *you* have the strong parental voice with the children. Note the word is "strong" — not overbearing. I have, at times, stooped to such an extreme in these matters. The end result is always the same: a bruised maternal ego, frightened or embarrassed children (depending on their ages), sullen obedience at best.

I am assuming that in your house it is the parents or parent who lead and the children who follow in whatever comfortable way your family has worked out. Keeping in mind that you and your spouse have made the decision to introduce home family prayer to the family in such a way as to enlist the children's support, it is important to be clear that the *decision* has been made. It is only the *implementation* of that decision which needs to be discussed. Indeed, do all the explaining you think necessary but keep this fact in the forefront: we are doing this because we love you and we think it is important for our family. Stress the united "we" as much as possible.

With very young children there will be little need for discussion of any kind. They are tractable and follow the parental lead as a matter of course. Besides, it is exciting and neat to be doing something with Mom and Dad and all the brothers and sisters or cousins or friends. You need only be careful not to overtire these little ones by making the sessions too long or beyond their understanding. Even the youngest baby can participate in family prayer if only by physical presence. Lying in a carriage or playpen or on a cozy lap, the youngest member of the family is present as the rest of the family prays and reads and talks. This will not be lost on the rest of them and will give your prayer a true family feeling.

There is no reason to insist that your prayers and Scripture readings always be done with the entire family together. At the time we started, our family divided neatly into a younger group and an older group between nine and twelve. Obviously the younger ones could not be expected to show much understanding of what the older children were doing, and the older ones would have been bored silly by the picture books and simple prayers of the "babies." There will be plenty of opportunity to combine the several age factions in your family and do something together in the form of home prayer. Just do not feel compelled to do so all the time.

The older children

Pre-teens and adolescents present different problems which need to be dealt with on a different level. When I talk about adolescents, I refer to very young teens. By the time young people are pushing eighteen, they are close enough to adulthood that any cooperation you get from them will be in the form of a gift. Younger teens and ten to twelve-year olds are under parental authority to a much greater degree. Certainly involve all your older children in the planning stages. Let them talk about "How should we do this?" but not "Will we do this?" That decision has already been made. Let them know that their cooperation is expected, their input appreciated. Our oldest child was twelve when we tried our first home prayer experience. Had he been much older I think I would have approached him somewhat as I did my husband, appealing for his help and partnership in bringing this new tradition into our home.

Over the years you and your spouse may have developed a strategy for dealing with your children during such times as these when new and perhaps not completely delightful things must be introduced into their lives for one good reason or another. Brace yourself for a certain amount of foot-dragging by your older children. After all, some of their free time will be invested in this. What you are about to embark upon may be quite different from anything that goes on in their friends' homes. At this age being different, even slightly, is suspect.

You may find yourself in a situation where your older children are rebelling loudly and clearly in full view of the younger ones. Do not, in a moment of frustration, allow these older ones to infringe on the rights of their younger siblings to learn and enjoy the prayers and rituals which will become part of their tradition. It is much too easy to blurt out, "OK, that's it! Don't come to the table for the Seder meal. Sleep through church on Sundays. You want to eat like a pig from a trough? You can't wait for grace? Go ahead! I've had it with you!"

Younger children are eagle-eyed to see how their older siblings react to new family situations, and often follow their lead. The words of an older brother or sister can carry considerable weight. Let the older ones vent their opposition and grievances with you in private. Insist on quiet cooperation in front of the younger ones. Nothing undermines your efforts so effectively as older children scowling or smirking their way

14

through home prayer or Bible readings.

Being approached as part of the adult team can go far to defuse rebellion. When we approached our older child this way, we were not just giving lip-service to our need for his cheerful cooperation. We did need his help and we got it, sometimes cheerfully and sometimes not. You and your spouse will negotiate your older children's cooperation or simply insist on it, according to your particular family dynamics.

Teens and even pre-teens are often in a state of happy pessimism. They constantly complain about everything but are happy being outwardly miserable. Just because one of yours is going through a period of flux and is in an itchy, pessimistic mood is no reason to allow him to push that attitude onto a younger child.

If, as a single parent, you have chosen a friend or some member of your extended family as a partner, and if your partner has children close to your older children in age, so much the better. Your older ones will be more inclined to go along with Christian rituals for the home, Scripture reading and prayers if others their age are involved.

The Outsiders

All right. You have negotiated with your spouse or teamed up with an adult friend or made the decision to try it alone. You have dealt successfully with the various children, young and old. What about the outside world? What about the playmate who happens to be at your house for dinner and gives you big eyes as you say grace? What about the relatives who spend Christmas Eve at your house and frankly find your Scripture reading and prayers quite silly, an intrusion on Santa's scene — and say so in loud voices in full hearing of your impressionable young children? Grown people could never be that insensitive you say? Think again. They can be and they sometimes are.

Your parents, in-laws, adult brothers and sisters have religious convictions of their own. Sometimes they have non-religious convictions. They handle their family life differently.

Seeing your family involved in rituals, prayers and Scripture, they may be happy for you, appalled at what you are doing or anything in between. Grandparents especially may be very uncomfortable with the idea of taking God out of church and bringing Him home. This discomfort sometimes manifests itself in strange ways. Perfectly lovely grandparents or sweet-tempered aunts and uncles can become quite indignant if they perceive what you are doing as breaking the traditions they grew up with.

Pay them no mind. Having set your goals and thoughtfully, prayerfully rearranged your priorities, be careful not to allow someone else's priorities to interfere. You may owe guests some sort of explanation, but that's all. If relatives insist on undermining your endeavors even after you have explained your plans and goals, you have several choices. Depending on how close your extended family is and how often you get together, you may want to pull back on some of the special gatherings. If, for example, Christmas Eve is always celebrated at your house and everyone comes to watch the kids hang stockings, inform the relatives that this year you will be reading the Bible and saying some special prayers and singing some songs together. Invite them to join you if they feel comfortable with what you are doing, or wait until you are finished with your special service before dropping in. There will be plenty of time for stocking hanging later after this more important part of the Christmas celebration is finished.

Perhaps your mother comes over often to help with evening chores and the children's bedtimes. If she is obviously put off by your nightly Bible reading or prayers, ask her to bake some cookies or sort laundry while you and the children have a quiet time together with Scripture or prayers.

This is your home, your children, your spouse. No one outside your immediate family has the right to dictate their feelings in your home.

The Bible on the Shelf

Getting into the Bible:

Of all our responsibilities as parents in a Christian home, Bible reading is probably the most slighted. If we bother at all, we tend to read *about* the Bible, choosing books which we consider easier, more understandable. Remember, only several generations ago reading and studying Scripture was as much a part of our American culture as reading the newspaper is today. The Bible often was used by the settlers of this country as a spelling book, reader and a source of guidance and spiritual refreshment. Many a family would not pass an evening without some Scripture.

With several children in the family including pre-schoolers and perhaps a baby, it is difficult to sit down to dinner all together. Do I expect you to believe that you can get all these people to sit still for regular Bible reading? If you go about it with plenty of patience and planning ... yes!

Several years ago when I was struggling to get our family started in a Scripture reading ritual, I spent a lot of time searching through various books for guidance and inspiration. Actually, I was hoping someone somewhere would tell me that it could be done, had been done and would show me exactly how to do it. My search uncovered numerous books dealing with different parts of the Bible text, explaining the meaning of Scripture. I found maps of the Holy Land and dictionaries especially written to familiarize me with Biblical terms. The closest I came to the guidance I needed was in Mary Reed Newland's *The Family and the Bible* (regrettably now out of print, but if you are ever lucky enough to unearth this little gem in a used book shop snatch it up and carry it home!). I've read it several times and my only disappointment is that Mrs. Newland spends only a few chary pages describing her family's experience in getting started with Scripture reading. Yet here is a mother of seven who had actually accomplished what so many of us yearn to do.

Goals: Why the Bible?

Why the Bible? Why struggle when there are other, much easier ways to sooth the parental conscience? Your family is probably fairly reliable as far as church attendance is concerned. We can assume most Sunday schools teach the kids Scripture along with the basics of the faith. If you believed that was enough you would have closed this chapter by now.

Sunday schools and church attendance are all to the good, but they just aren't enough. Once a week doesn't form a person for a lifetime of discipleship. Scripture reading (and understanding) clarifies, shapes and changes the fabric of our lives into a certain form, into the kingdom ethic.

You give your children as many of the learning tools as you can afford. While they are still very young you give them puzzles, story books, bright colored toys. As they grow older you are happy to provide good books, special tutoring in difficult subjects, typewriters, calculators, a garden variety of lessons (swimming, dancing, music, etc.) and always through

18

the years your personal help and encouragement. If not carried to extremes, this is good and generous and helpful. All these tools train and mold a child to fit into adult society in a purely functional way. But, in the midst of this giving and guiding and nurturing sometimes we forget the most important preparation of all — the spiritual growth of the soul. To give a child material things and parental support alone is like giving a carpenter the tools to build a house but not the blueprint. Your children learn diverse skills on the long road into adulthood, but, without that all-important blueprint, those skills may be wasted and the house of the spirit may not get built at all.

The Bible is the best blueprint for a Christian life. It spans the range of human emotions and experience. It is filled with ordinary and some not-so-ordinary people living out their lives while interacting with their God.

I am not here to convince you that reading the Bible will enrich your life and the lives of your children. If you are not willing to exert a lot of effort in that direction, then close this chapter and go on to something else, because the commitment must originate within you, not be induced by a convincing book or article.

Timing: That all-important ingredient

You know how deadly poor timing can be to the simplest family plans. A picnic or Christmas tree trimming evening can be ruined by an excess of spontaneity if you are dealing with several children of different ages. If the baby missed her nap, or your toddler had three peas and a cracker for lunch and is ravenous, or your older child came home from school piled with homework, you had *better* consider these things and work around them in your planning. If you don't, the nice outing or family evening you planned will degenerate into a hair-raising scene. The same rules apply for family Scripture reading.

Sometimes it happens that in the first fine glow of a new experience we tend to become larger than life size. In our great urge to push our family onto the pathway to God we instead become the obstacles along that path. It is best to go slow at first. Look around you. Consider what you have to work with, what you must work around.

If you plan to schedule Bible reading once a week or every other week, look for that evening which will engender the least amount of teeth-gnashing from the family over missed television shows. Never schedule your Bible evening to compete with Scout meetings or basketball practice. Trying to duck around the television schedule will present a bigger challenge. Modern technology can come to your aid here if you own a VCR. It is easy enough to tape a show and save it for another time. This will free you from the complete domination of the television schedule. A VCR, however, is an expensive little toy. If you are not ready to make that kind of investment there are other ways to work Scripture reading into your evenings.

If the kids are glued to a game show every Tuesday evening at 7:30, leave that time alone. It does not matter that Bible reading is more important than the show. Of course it is, but why ask for trouble and tantrums at the start by deliberately substituting something they are unfamiliar with for something they look forward to all week? Get together with your spouse or other adult partner on this. The two of you will look over the TV schedule, set limits, make choices and then present your decision to the children in your own preferred way. It might be a good idea to check with the older children for their opinions of the best night. The less mutiny you have in this quarter, the smoother things will go.

Begin with fifteen or twenty minutes maximum as your Bible time. Maximum. Very young children will find it difficult to concentrate even this long. You can always increase the time as you go along. This is preferable to whittling down the sessions if you've started with a long hour. The effect of that can be demoralizing.

This brings up a point often questioned: what age is best for beginning Scripture reading with children? If we waited until they were well along in school, say in the fourth grade, wouldn't the Scriptures, with their difficult language and subtle teaching, be easier to understand?

No doubt the children will be more comfortable with the text and language at that age, but you will pay a price if you decide to wait too long. If you are living with a child above the age of ten, I'm sure you've realized that as children grow older, they tend to yield less graciously to parental suggestions. What you will gain in maturity and ability by waiting until your children are older you may lose in compliance and delight.

If you find you want to read the Bible more than once a week, or even nightly, the same rules apply: a few verses each evening at a time when the very youngest children can be easily managed and you are not taking any special activity away from anyone. I found that the time right before bed worked well for us when we first began. The children were younger (and fewer). Bedtime was earlier. Then, as the incumbent children grew older and new ones were added to the family, I divided them into two groups according to age. Now the younger ones are still amenable to hearing some Scripture right before lights out at night, but the older ones do better with the Bible reading coming at the end of their homework time. They read some Scripture individually and once or twice a month we all get together for reading and some discussion. This monthly family Bible reading works best for us on early Sunday evenings. The children know that time has been set aside especially for this purpose and they have the weekend to do homework and wind up any projects. This way one or several do not turn up with a major science report or test to study for right at Bible time, as could easily happen on a weekday evening. I keep a large calendar on the kitchen bulletin board with nice fat spaces to write in each day's appointments. Our Bible night is penciled in just as any other important appointment would be.

With your younger ones you might want to introduce the Bible by telling them that they are going to have an extra bedtime story from a special book. You will know how to get across whatever background information you feel your · children need about the Bible. I told mine it was a little like a story book about some interesting people and that it was special because it was God's word. We began with a good hardbound illustrated children's Bible and varied this with Bible story books from the town library.

With older children I would start right in with the family Bible. There is no substitute for the Word of God and the sooner the children are able to read directly from an adult Bible the better.

Nowhere is it written in stone that we must begin with Genesis and carry on right through to the final book. Begin where you like. Read as much as you like. You can pick up a Bible study guide in most bookstores. Your public library may have some. Mine did. It will be a great help if you are feeling uncertain as to what to read and how to read it. This type of guide book should also give you enough background to help put whatever you are reading into historical perspective. I cannot emphasize enough how much easier and more pleasurable (to say nothing of profitable) your Bible reading sessions will be if you rely on these little guide books. They usually set up readings, questions, answers and discussion topics for both the Old Testament and the New Testament, to be used as you go along.

As we went through the Bible with the older children, we found some chapters tedious. Rather than dragging through each and every word, we skipped large sections of the book, going on to something which held their interest, and which we considered to be more important at that time. For my own comfort I familiarized myself with some biblical history to help flesh out and embellish the Scripture reading sessions.

We did our Bible reading on a big bed, snuggled under a warm comforter in winter, or out on the breezy back porch in summer. With the little ones, if we were simply reading a few verses without discussion,I would sit on their beds and read as they lay there and drowsed in that cradled twilight just before sleep. Then off went the light and they would say their prayers, followed by a good-night kiss and hug the last thing.

If you choose to establish Scripture reading as a bedtime ritual, keep in mind that reading the Bible should not take the place of any of the regular bedtime ceremonies at your house. These are always important to very young children. If your child's bedtime rituals involve a snack, a bath, a story, a drink, a kiss, a back rub or whatever else you have evolved to insure peace and security, don't skip any of it in favor of Scripture reading.

In any family there will be evenings when the parents are too tired or too busy or on the run and cannot fulfill all of the rituals their children have come to associate with bedtime. Something must be skipped. When you are still in the beginning stages of reading Scripture with your children, don't try substituting Bible reading for their accustomed and cherished rites. Once the Scripture reading has actually evolved into a ritual, a special storytime with you and something they anticipate, you are free to make changes and substitutions as you like.

Schedules

In a family full of active people it is easy to fall behind in something as tenuous as Bible reading. After all, how much can it hurt if you let it go tonight and tomorrow and even for two weeks? There are so many pressing demands, and bedtime is fraught with the common tensions of winding up a busy day. Urgent duties call and at times keeping up with the little ones' Scripture reading or supervising the older children's reading seems to lose some of its importance. There will be times and circumstances which will tempt you to skip a reading now and again, especially in summer when the children seem to be going in five different directions.

You will know when you've skipped too many and it is time to get back on schedule. You should not be haphazard about your Bible reading schedule, but do be flexible. Be patient with yourself.

Do your best to stay on schedule while getting into the Bible readings until they become ingrained in your family pattern. If you've been consistent when you first introduced Scripture reading into your family's schedule, your diligence will pay off later. Once the readings become an established routine, skipping won't throw everyone off track quite so easily. Do not berate yourself too harshly if you do have to let the scheduled readings go now and then.

If you are on your own with Bible reading, either as a single parent, or at the request of your spouse, there are a number of ways to handle the scheduling. Your private Scripture reading, that which you do often or nightly with your own children, needs to be kept as simple as possible. Keep discussion brief at these times and keep the material down to just one verse or at the most two for younger children. These are the bedtime readings, the few words at the end of the day, no less important because they are few. Remember you are on your own here. If you begin with a full chapter *and* discussion will you be willing (or able) to keep it going on a nightly or even a weekly basis? If you are partnering with another adult not in your household for the longer Bible reading sessions, there is no reason to elongate these daily or weekly bedtime readings which fall to you alone.

Actually, I found that after the older children had become comfortable with Scripture reading, they were willing to read a Scripture verse to the younger ones at bedtime occasionally. I let them take over for me once in a while if my evening schedule was very tight.

Hopefully you have found a partner to help in the scheduling and planning of your monthly or bi-weekly Scripture reading sessions which include several verses and lengthier discussion. Plan these Scripture sessions with care, utilizing the assistance of Bible study guides. Remember that these are learning sessions for the entire family.

When to begin

Another aspect of this fledgling period of getting into Scripture reading with your family is the question of when to begin. What is the best time of year? Summer? Christmas? Easter season? Fall? Spring? Is one season easier than another? I think so.

Summer, at first glance, looks promising. The children are out of school and their time is not taken up with lessons and after-school activities. Bedtimes are more flexible. Groups, clubs, committees are less active, freeing up some time for you. So it would seem, but the reality is quite different.

If your children, like mine, span a large age group, nobody is doing the same thing or can be found in one place during the long summer days and evenings. One may have gone fishing, another swimming. The pre-schooler may be involved with a bevy of friends by the digging hole in the back yard, while his twelve-year-old brother is wheeling out of the driveway bound for a long bike trip. Mealtimes are less structured in summer. The older ones beg for permission to join neighborhood friends under the street light after dark for games. My husband has to be physically dragged out of his garden, even after sunset.

In summer the family is scattered. You can try to compensate for this by insisting on a set dinner time whenever possible and by continuing to do some pre-planned things together as a group. Weekly Bible reading can be one of these. Continuing an established routine is one thing, but introducing a new dimension to family living during this free-spirited season is not a good idea for most families with more than two children.

One exception to this might be your vacation trip. If you are vacationing in a quiet, out of the way area such as a cottage along a lonely beach or a deep woods campground, so much the better. Here you can set your own pace, live free of schedules and have your children around most of the day and evening. Now, away from television and little league, you can slowly introduce them to Scripture reading a little each day or every other day. Here you may even find time for your own very important quietness, time to read the Bible, time to think and to pray.

Suppose that instead of a secluded vacation you are about to take off on a two-week jaunt of sight seeing and visiting in a far distant locality. If your destination is several days' car ride away consider the possibilities. You are being blessed with a nearly perfect setting for reading and discussion. There you are with the family packed into the car with five or six hours of enforced togetherness ahead of you. The younger ones are already fighting over who will sit next to the windows. Engage their attention with a "Bible break." Schedule a half hour each traveling day for Bible reading and discussion. You will want to break this half hour into fifteen minute sessions with perhaps an hour or more in between.

If your spouse is at the wheel and you are in the back seat reading with the older ones, maybe deep in a good discussion, the driver might entertain the younger ones in the front with a quiet road game or a story. Again, set your goals. Prepare ahead of time and *be flexible*.

Don't believe for a minute that you can just bring along the Bible and everything will fall into place. After some years of Scripture reading with the family it might work out this way, or it may do for the younger children, but not for the older ones. Familiarize yourself with the chapters or verses you will be reading together *before* the trip. Have some questions ready to keep the discussion lively. Write them down if it makes you more comfortable. The more you put in writing the less you'll be carrying around in your overburdened memory right before vacation time when winding up things on your job and getting the family organized takes all your time and strength. Rely on your guide book, the handy little book we talked about earlier that takes you step-by-step through chapter and verse.

I have found it helpful to bring along a small tape recorder. I prepare the tapes at home and we play them as we drive along. Always included are the verses we are studying when vacation time rolls around. Sometimes I tape some favorite songs or some questions which are sure to stimulate a good discussion. For some reason young children consider it a novelty to listen to tapes and their attention stays focused. I make different tapes for different age groups. While the younger ones are listening, the older ones can become involved as they wish.

There are, of course, Scripture readings which the whole family can study together and these are especially nice to share in the small enclosed space of the car as we cruise along.

If I were starting into family Bible reading now, I think I would visit the religious book stores and buy some ready-made tapes of Bible readings. I was not aware of such tapes being on the market years ago when our family was getting into Scripture reading (See Resource Chapter).

If vacation time seems right to you for introducing the family to Scripture reading here is one way you might go about it:

First, set some goals. Where do you want to begin? The Old Testament? The New Testament? Bible stories from other books? A lot will depend on the ages of your children and your own degree of comfort and familiarity with the Bible.

With very young children you may want to start out with Bible stories from a nice, colorfully illustrated children's Bible. My feeling is that the sooner we can wean children away from exclusive reliance on the picture Bible stories and into the real Scriptures the better.

How much to read each day? Set aside some time for discussion and questions the children might have. Half an hour traveling time each day seems right. Remember, traveling time is not like regular time at home or anywhere else. There are a lot of hours to fill. While you might get resistance if the sessions go too long at home, usually the novelty of a trip coupled with the fact that all of you are confined in a small space without much to do puts Scripture reading in a new light. Just knowing that something is scheduled for half an hour a day can be welcome on a long trip. Let the family know that at home and during your vacation stay this half hour will be reduced.

Secondly, prepare yourself as thoroughly as your time and temperament allow. It is a good idea to have some prior familiarity with the background of the chapter you will be reading. Here is where the handy Scripture guide comes in. Use it to help you understand enough about what you are reading to be able to answer the children's questions and enrich the discussion. Use it to help you select the chapters and verses to be read. Use it for historical perspective, to help you better grasp the context in which those verses were written.

The "Bible break" might be just the right time for a snack.

27

If you have pre-recorded the readings, so much the better. You can slip the tape into the recorder or tape deck, settle the baby with a bottle and break out juice and cookies for the other travelers. Now, sit back and relax and enjoy listening and talking together.

How does a single parent handle all this? That depends on your resources. If you will be sharing your traveling vacation with a close friend who is also single with children, get together for some pre-trip planning.

Decide well in advance who will buy or make the tapes, which chapters to cover each traveling day, which of you is responsible for background information for these. Divide all this as fairly as you will divide the driving time. The important thing is, of course, to talk it *all* over with your friend in advance and come to a complete understanding. If your goals are not compatible, forget the whole thing and begin your family Bible reading another time. If your friend is less than enthusiastic about vacation time blending well with Scripture reading, be aware of this before you set off on the trip together. Shelve the whole idea until your family is home again.

Fall seems like a good time to introduce family Scripture reading, Christian rituals and family prayer. Your days become more scheduled and predictable once school begins. Of course, along with the school season comes the usual grab-bag of committee meetings and after school activities, most of which involve you or your spouse in some way if your children are not old enough to drive. Each meeting or basketball practice attended requires some sort of transportation compromise by you — car-pooling if you are lucky, or playing taxi driver all by yourselves. Remember that every activity outside the home is that much less time for the family to spend together.

If you have made the decision to begin your family Scripture reading in the fall and you have some weeks of summer left to pull it all together, start by looking around and determining what you have to work with. Where can you make changes that will loosen your schedule, giving you some time to bring the people in your house into contact with one another?

Start with your own time. How many committees do you serve on? Just what is your after-work schedule like? What can you pare away to free some time for other priorities? How much of your time is involved with carting the kids around to lessons, activities, sports events?

One late afternoon in November during the heyday of our children's involvement in after-school activities, I was driving a carpool-load of six-year olds to dancing class when we happened to pass my husband's car filled with Cub Scouts, headed for the bowling alley in the opposite direction. Our Beth stopped giggling and bouncing on the back seat with her friends long enough to glance out the car window at her father. "Mommy," she said, hanging over the front seat and breathing down my neck, "was that Daddy?"

Now I did not think for a minute that this child could not recognize her own father, but her words made me consider something that had been scratching uncomfortably at my mind for some time. When I glanced at my husband through the windshields that separated us, I saw not my usual mental image of the man who shares my home, but a tired face doggedly making his appointed car-pool rounds, bound by inflexible schedules and chained to the steering wheel by the children's activities.

That evening I reflected on the soundness of what we were doing with our time. We talked about it, streamlined the children's schedules and vowed to never again get so deeply mired in the after-school racket.

Be aware of the heavy load of activities, yours as well as the children's, that almost automatically comes with the territory of the school year. Set some carefully thought out priorities for your time and theirs. It is a good idea to wait until about a month into the school year. By that time schedules are settled and homework has stabilized, giving you some idea of how much evening time you have at your disposal. Also, by then the days are growing shorter and twilight draws an early curtain over your evening, bringing the children indoors to you.

Whatever your choice, whatever season or situation you

find easiest for your introduction to Bible reading with the family, the important thing is not to put it off once your decision has been made. If you are in the middle of winter and find yourself ready to plunge in, then by all means, plunge! Do not wait around for spring or fall or some other illusive, ideal time. There is no ideal time except that which you determine with your own enthusiasm.

A Bible evening

You have scrutinized your schedule and pared away some unwanted activities. You have read the TV guide with your spouse or partner and have circled a date on your kitchen calendar for Bible reading. Let us say this is a first for your family. The children have heard Scripture at church and Sunday school but not at home.

Sometime before the evening scheduled for Scripture reading, look over the selected reading. Now is the time to use that Bible guide book you bought a while back. Become comfortable with the reading and have some questions in mind in case the discussion falters.

Talk to your older children privately. Tell them the date and time the family will be gathering. Write it on *their* calendars for good measure.

It would be best if someone other than you took over the actual reading of the Bible as soon as possible. This might be your spouse or one of the older children. You are already looked upon as the planner, the instigator, the leader in all this. The sooner you can turn these roles over to someone else in the family who can handle them, the better. If you are always the one to plan and schedule, read and lead the prayer or discussion, the rest of your people will happily sit back and enjoy the show. They need to get actively involved, and fast!

Your partner, if he or she is willing, might share the leadership role: reading, planning, talking with the children about what you've read together. This is especially good for the older children in the house to observe.

Perhaps in your house, as in ours, the planning will always be your share. Things just evolved that way for us. I plan, sometimes with my husband's help and advice. Then, the rest of the responsibilities are meted out to the others. Someone reads. Someone else leads a prayer or lights the candles. By the time you have been reading the Bible together for a number of years, the planning will be minimal. Once these rituals become traditions they seem to flow on their own very nicely.

Prayer, Family Style

"Only he can live well who knows how to pray well."
St. Augustine

The Judeo-Christian tradition presumes an ongoing two-way, communication with God. We who ride this planet for a lifetime take this presumption so casually! When we pray we communicate, attend to the creator of our world, our universe. I suppose if our minds were really able to internalize this vast idea we would be so awed that prayer might be impossible. Yet, our Creator himself extends the invitation:

"And all these things whatsoever ye shall ask in prayer, believing, ye shall receive" (Mt. 21:22).

"Ask and it shall be given you; seek and you shall find; knock and it shall be opened to you" (Mt. 7:7).

If we are to be a prayerful people, communication with God must begin early in our lives. As adults we bring to our new

32

tradition of family prayer the habits and hang-ups of our childhood, what we learned about praying, what we resented and even what we vowed to forget. This chapter will focus on the process of setting up a prayer tradition in your family rather than on the purpose, type or content of prayer. Where you disagree with my methods or even with the prayers involved, modify and fit the ideas to your family and your personal concept of prayer.

Grace: the easiest prayer

Without doubt one of the easiest forms of prayer to introduce to your family is grace at meals. Whether you choose to say grace before or after meals, whether you decide upon one meal a day or three, the family will more easily accept prayer at mealtimes than at any other time of day. One of the reasons for this is simple logistics. You are all together at one time in one place for the purpose of eating. The prayer is added on as a part of this gathering. You have no need to pull your people away from their work, their play.

There is another reason for the ready acceptance of saying grace at meals. You are tying into an established practice, rather than breaking new ground with an untried or unusual prayer tradition that might be greeted with suspicion. Most people who have grown up in the Judeo-Christian tradition have said some form of table grace at least for the great feasts of the year — Christmas, Thanksgiving, Easter. Grace is not an altogether unfamiliar prayer.

Children, young or old, tend to want to skid in at mealtimes, grab a quick hamburger, toss on some fries, wash the whole thing down with a cold drink and be off again to their exciting and exacting world. In every family with growing children, and possibly two wage-earners' schedules, there are meals like this once in a while. When they become the routine rather than the exception, it is time to re-evaluate. It is time to take a look at what the children are learning about priorities, about jumping off the fast track once in a while and giving a thought to where we are going.

Grace at mealtimes forces us to the awareness that we sit

at a table about to enjoy the bounties (be it only cereal and milk) that our Lord has provided. Our awareness of blessings extends to the idea that we should be thankful for the very fact that we are able, physically and mentally, to provide this food, whether grown in our back yard or bought at the local grocery store with hard-earned money. This is not lost on the children in the family; it only needs to be pointed out in our prayer. It also answers the inevitable question that will come up if any of your children are younger than six: How come we thank God for this dinner if Mom cooked it?

This table prayer, simple or elaborate, is the staying hand that reaches out to our growing family and says, "Stop! Think and be aware of God."

Simple though they may be, the words of thanks before a meal elevate us to an awareness of our relationship with our Maker. Unlike cattle feeding at a trough, we are a people made in the image of God, who take time to be aware of His presence in our lives and at our table. Prayer does not bring God into our lives or our presence. He is always with us. Prayer, instead, brings us into the awareness or presence of God who has been there all along but who gets generally ignored in the rush of tax statements and soccer practice.

We began our family prayer rituals with table grace for the reasons mentioned above and also because it is the one prayer that, in its simplest form, we all say together, putting the focus on the family group rather than any one individual.

Planning

If you read the introductory chapter of this book, you must be aware of the importance placed on letting your spouse or adult partner in on all planning at every stage of establishing new spiritual family traditions. Family prayer is no exception. Even though you will probably begin with an easy prayer like table grace, don't use the element of surprise. It is best to prepare the children ahead of time. Do not jump up from the table one evening just as the family is reaching for the chicken and the potatoes and shout out, "Stop! Don't anyone eat anything. We are going to say grace!" Imagine the reaction of your family! I don't have to imagine, for this is how I did it. This was my family's introduction to table grace. I can only be thankful our children were all young at the time and don't remember Mom's pronouncement. My husband does remember, however, and my ill-timed broadcast has gone down in family lore as "Mom's fall from grace."

Your children, depending upon their ages may put the question: Why grace? Why now? No one has bothered about thanking God for much up to now. How come we are all of a sudden getting so holy? Your answer, couched in your own words of course, is simple: All good things must have a beginning. Better late, better now, than never.

Having made the decision to say grace and having informed the children, you will need to plan a time when the family will most likely gather together for a meal. Is breakfast the only meal you can count on for all of you? Good. What better way to start the day than to thank God for the bacon, the eggs and muffins as well as the new day unfolding before you? In our church we sing a hymn that contains the words, "This is the day the Lord has made. Let us rejoice and be glad." These simple words form a beautiful morning prayer and a thought to carry throughout the day as we scurry off to jobs and to schools.

Simple or complex, breakfast grace will only work in your family if the morning scene at your house is relatively sane and you can count on a gathering of the clan. Our morning scene is so rushed and confusing we have not ever attempted to say a family prayer at breakfast. Both adults rush off to jobs on weekday mornings. The children go to four different schools. People fly downstairs to grab toast and cereal and spill juice. Cats jump up on counters and the dogs scratch at the back door. No one has time to give "the day the Lord has made" more than a passing glance through the smudged kitchen windows. On weekends breakfast is eliminated, as the various children and adults trail downstairs intermittently, from the earliest cartoon enthusiast to the noon riser.

Perhaps your family, like ours, will concentrate on getting together for the evening meal. Picture everyone gathered around the table. *Everyone* includes the adult who happens to be serving the meal. Join the family for prayer without jumping up to turn down the oven or bring bread to the table. The children, ever alert to your example, are quick to see that grace is not important enough to merit your complete attention. This will leave a lasting impression with them that all your subsequent excuses and explanations cannot budge.

Perhaps you would like to hold hands or bow your heads or look at each other while you pray. If you were in the habit of saying a table grace in your childhood home you may want to use it now. If not, there are helpful books of table graces available (see Resources).

There is a paradox about table grace that usually goes unnoticed until it is upon you. Most families start out using a memorized short prayer. This prayer is easy to remember and usually continues unchanged for years (if not forever!). The danger is that, although it may be an easy prayer to say, it is a difficult prayer to attend to after much repetition. A friend of mine tells this story of grace at meals during his childhood:

His father, as head of the family, was the only one permitted to say grace at their table. No exceptions were allowed. Over the years the prayer had become so hackneyed that no one paid the slightest attention to the words, the meaning behind those words, or the fact that this was a time of communication with their God. In fact, my friend recalls that as time went by, his father began to repeat the words of the prayer (always the same one; no exceptions allowed here either) faster and faster each evening until the actual prayer was reduced to a three or four second mumble which had lost all significance for the rest of the family. My friend and his brother would surreptitiously count the time it took their father to say grace. Each evening at dinner they would finger-tap the seconds under cover of the hanging tablecloth, hoping their father would beat his own record.

There is nothing difficult about avoiding such meaningless repetition in your table grace. Buy or take out of your library a book on grace for meals. Some of these books have grace for holidays and mealtime prayers for many special occasions such as birthdays and namedays.

Try using Scripture for your table grace. A few verses from the Psalms or the gospels quietly read and quietly attended to are a good beginning for any meal. Bible verses can (with some maneuvering by the adults present) lead to interesting table-talk during the meal as well. I don't mean to imply that your conversation at meals needs to be a teaching mechanism or necessarily a theological discussion. People in biblical times were very different. They talked differently and dressed differently. Presented in the right way, in a casual non-pressured story-telling manner, these ancient times and people make fascinating conversation. I can remember a period in our family when the dinner conversation deteriorated to rock band lingo by the teens (which no one over thirty understood) and loud complaints by the younger group about whatever food was being served. Somewhere toward the end of the meal someone was bound to ask what animal we were eating and what part of it was sitting on the meat platter at the moment. We discovered that one way to dislodge this unappetizing habit was to hold the conversation, at least through part of the meal, to something reasonable. Reading a Bible verse during grace and talking about it gets dinner conversation off to a good start, comparatively anyway.

As you and your family become comfortable with saying or reading table grace and begin to get involved in family prayer evenings, someone in the family may want to write a table grace for all to pray together. Sometimes children get more easily involved in this than older teens or adults. I remember a Thanksgiving grace our Noelle wrote when she was seven. It catalogued each and every blessing this family had ever received. We sat around holding hands and listening to her read her prayer for what seemed like half an hour to the rest of us, but was actually less than five minutes. I still have that early attempt of hers copied carefully in my book of table graces. There are things I would part with far easier than that little prayer.

Eventually the time may come when one of you will want to pray aloud and spontaneously before a meal. Remember that it takes a long time, an open atmosphere and a lot of trust to pray aloud in front of others. Please don't *assign* that role to anyone, including your spouse or partner, unless that person suggests it or you can clearly see that he or she would like to try spontaneous prayer but is hesitant to ask. Forcing anyone to pray aloud in front of a silent group (even a family group) is deadly. Family climate is very important here. Can you visualize a spontaneous prayer being said by anyone at the childhood table of my friend?

Dolores Curran in discussing Catholic prayer, points out, "The closest many of us came to praying together was the family rosary which is essentially a private prayer shared. Often we knelt back to back and were taught not to look at one another. It takes a great leap to go from that kind of childhood prayer into a casual spontaneous kind of shared prayer around the table or in front of the fireplace" (Dolores Curran, *And Then God Made Families*). Indeed it does. Unlike Jewish families, we Christians have no great tradition of family feast days and prayers celebrated at home. We need to begin slowly and, most of all, be patient with ourselves and with our families.

From your family's decision to say a prayer of thanks at mealtimes can grow a tradition of saying special grace for your personal family occasions such as birthdays, anniversaries, namedays, as well as the big holidays throughout the year. Families bring together their own times of rejoicing in their own unique ways. For example we have a birthday grace in our family which is said on or as close as possible to the birthday. During the Advent season we say a blessing for the Advent wreath each Sunday and a daily prayer involving the Jesse tree. When the children were all home we said a prayer each Saturday before dinner thanking God for our week and asking Him to bless each of us and help us to remember the significance of the Sabbath. In November we pray for our dead. During Lent we say prayers to help signify this special season.

Not all these prayers came to us ready-made. Most of them evolved out of a need and developed over a period of time as our prayer life grew and changed. I have included them in this book to use as a springboard for individualizing your own family prayers and tailoring them to your special celebrations.

Sunday Grace

We have evolved a very simple but effective tradition of bread-breaking which goes along with Sunday dinner at our house. After the prayer or Bible verse my husband breaks a small piece of bread, holds it up and says, "Eat and remember the goodness of the Lord." After breaking off a small bit for himself, he passes the bread to the child or guest sitting next to him who in turn breaks off a small bit and passes the piece to the person next to him and so on around the table. The whole thing takes no longer than a minute or two. It is yet another way of holding Sunday, the Sabbath day, apart from the rest of the week. This small blessing adds something to our meal, a remembrance of who we are and why we are celebrating Sunday as different from the hectic work days of the week. Eat and remember.

Our Sunday grace is different in another respect. While during the week we usually stay with the memorized prayer for grace, we use Scripture for our grace on Sundays. As mentioned earlier, the psalms or the gospels lend themselves well to short readings at table. Other books of the Bible could be used just as well. Sometimes reading a part of whatever chapters were read during the church service that morning leads to good table talk. If nothing else, it brings to light which of us at least attempted to understand the sermon and which of us slept right through with our eyes open.

Sabbath Eve Grace

Moses warned his people thirty centuries ago to be on guard against their own successes, against forgetting their God from whom all their blessings have come. The very same warning applies today. How easy it is to forget our inherent human weakness when we have dominated nature, vanquished so many diseases, touched the surface of heavenly orbs and trod this earth as industrialized giants. The words of Moses have an uncomfortably familiar ring: "... then thy heart be lifted up, and thou forget the Lord thy God ... and thou say in thy heart: My power and the might of hand hath gotten me this wealth!" A weekly reminder that it is God to whom we owe thanks for our blessings is not amiss in any family.

In the Jewish tradition the Sabbath or *Shabbat* begins at sundown on Friday and ends on Saturday evening. Just as the sun begins to give way to the coming darkness, but before night is completely upon them, Jewish families usher in the *Shabbat*. They sing, pray, bless the children and wish each other a good Sabbath and a good week to come. They eat special foods and commemorate the occasion by using the good linens, china and silver.

For years I had been fascinated by this spiritual tradition, by the continuity it gave to time, counting the days of the week from Sabbath Eve to Sabbath Eve, like beads upon an endless string. I especially liked the ceremony being set at home around the family table rather than at church. All Christians trace their spiritual roots to their Jewish heritage. Why not, I asked myself, incorporate some of these beautiful Jewish traditions into our home? We did some research and changed some of the elements of the traditional Shabbat ritual to fit our family's needs. The main idea was to bring our weekly treadmill to a halt on the eve of the Sabbath, preparing ourselves for the coming of God's special day by stopping to put our lives into perspective and to take a good look at each other and appreciate what we saw.

By no means did we incorporate all or even a great deal of the Shabbat ritual of our Jewish friends. My intention was not to copy the ceremony with any degree of exactness. I wanted to bring into our home the *idea* of a breathing spell at the end of the week, a simple, short ceremony that would help us stop and remember our love for our God and for each other.

Our family had been saying table grace together for about a year when we decided to introduce the Sabbath eve grace. If you are interested in this special ritual it makes sense to get your family comfortable with saying grace at meals first. Again, as always, discussing your interests and plans with your spouse is paramount. If he or she has gone along with you in Bible reading, family prayers and table grace, you should have no problem in gathering support for this beautiful new ritual.

Depending on how your spouse reacts and what time constraints each of you has, you will either plan this prayer together or one of you will plan it and present it to the other. If you are a single parent you may want to team up with a friend or adult sibling (the same one you team with for Bible reading?) and pool your time, resources and kids. The precautions here are the same as those discussed in chapter two. Tread slowly at first. Think through your commitment carefully.

You may not want to use good silver, china and linens every week at the Saturday night meal. The important thing is to commemorate the family gathering. Holding down an outside job and contending with older teenagers who are often not at home makes it impossible for our family to gather together every Saturday evening. There are plenty of Saturday nights when we may be saying Sabbath Eve grace to a comparatively empty table, but that's part of the process of children growing up and away. Numbers are not important.

In any large and growing family there will be people missing at mealtimes for one good reason or another. There will be noise and spilled milk and at times flared tempers. We are living in a home, after all, not a tabernacle. Clean up the milk and referee the arguments. Quiet the baby with a carrot stick or a cracker. The thought is there. The effort is there and if you are patient and consistent, any ritual can become — after a time — a tradition. Don't get trapped into thinking that unless all your people and your setting can be managed perfectly, you may as well forget the Sabbath Eve grace altogether. Better to enjoy take-out pizza at the kitchen counter with the family focusing on God's blessing and on each other than to forego the prayers because you're too busy to bother with the trappings.

I will gladly share with you our prayers for Sabbathe Eve. Knowing the needs and tolerance of your own family, you can then make changes where necessary.

The first month or so that we involved our family in this special ritual, I used a white cloth and tried to make sure whomever set the table matched glasses and china for a more uniform effect. Since Saturday is a very busy day for us, the food varied according to what happened to be easiest to prepare. Candles are essential and it is especially nice to eat after dark to better enjoy the candle glow. This is easier to do in winter than in summer, but even when used before sunset, candles have a quieting effect. We sit together at the table and when everyone is quiet and ready, I light the candles and say:

Let us welcome the Sabbath with candles and prayer.

God, our Father, come into our home tonight and bless our family gathered here. Help us to put aside the cares of the week and prepare for your Sabbath. We thank you for each other, for your constant love and care. Help us to walk closer with you in the coming week.

Then my husband says:

May the Lord bless you and keep you. May the Lord make His face to shine upon you and give you peace.

All of us say, "Amen."

We do not sing or pray in unison or prolong the meal as a celebration, as our Jewish friends do for their Sabbath Eve. We simply pause to remember that tomorrow is a special day. You can expand this grace in many ways. I can highly recommend a book by Siegel, Strassfeld and Strassfeld entitled *The First Jewish Catalog* if you are interested in learning about the very complicated and elaborate Jewish Sabbath Eve ritual and perhaps modifying it to meet your family's needs.

On or close to a person's birthday, we say a grace especially to commemorate that person and ask God to bless him or her. Anyone can read this grace, mother, father, one of the brothers or sisters. It is quite special to have a grandparent read it if the family is gathering for a birthday dinner. You can also have it duplicated and all read the grace together for the birthday person:

Father, we ask you to bless this child of yours today. Grant him/her the grace and wisdom to know your law and to walk

42

always in your light. Walk with him Lord, we pray.

Grant him a loving heart, and a strong will. Keep him safe from the corruption of the world. Be with him as he journeys to Your kingdom and when his days on earth are accomplished welcome him into paradise with you forever. We ask this in Jesus' name. Amen.

As I mentioned earlier, you may get a strong reaction to any or all of these prayer rituals and table graces from visitors. Not all the members of your extended family or even your friends are likely to understand or even approve of what you are doing. Don't let that bother you. Do as much explaining as you feel compelled to do and let the rest go. They may come around in time as your prayer traditions grow and take root in your family's spiritual life. Or they may always view what you do with suspicion. Does it really matter?

Father's Day Grace

Father's Day is a special day in our family. We read or say from memory a prayer before dinner on Father's Day:

Lord, bless this man whom You have entrusted as head of our home. Give him the wisdom to guide his children to Your kingdom. Give him the strength to provide for his family's needs. Give him the love and patience to be a helpmate to his wife. Help him to remember the words of the prophet Micah: 'This is what Yahweh asks of you: only this, to act justly, to love tenderly and to walk humbly with your God' (Micah 6:8). Amen.

Mother's Day Grace

Before serving and eating dinner on Mother's Day, which should be prepared at least in part by anyone other than the mother, we say this prayer:

Father, we ask Your blessings on the mother of this family. Give her strength to carry out her duties. Give her patience and love to guide her children. Help her to be a helpmate and an inspiration to her husband. We ask this in Jesus' name. Amen.

Since our family is nearly grown, many of the children

travel during the year as college vacations roll around. If someone is heading for far-off places we try to have a special meal the evening before that child leaves home. If grandparents, aunts, uncles or cousins are in the vicinity, they naturally are invited to see our traveler off. We say or read this grace before the evening meal:

Father, we ask you to bless this child of yours as she leaves her people to journey far from home. Protect her. Give her courage and the comfort of Your presence. Bring her safely home again. Amen.

Whether we call them prayer rituals or grace before meals, these simple prayers help to focus on the milestones in the lives of our family members. They remind us that God needs to be a presence in our homes, not a mystical Being who lives only in church. Because it is easier to gather a family around the table than anywhere else, these prayers take the form of grace in our family. Use them to gather your special people around your table.

Prayer, Family Style

Now that your family is comfortable praying together at the table before or after meals, you are ready to go on to, as Dolores Curran puts it, "prayer around the fireplace."

There is nothing spectacular about our family prayer gatherings. Once a week immediately after dinner, before anyone can scatter, we stack the dishes, put the food away and gather in the livingroom. After a short verbal scuffle over whose turn it is to light the candle, we sit or kneel on the rug. Although I don't believe in the formalized hands-together-and-back-straight kneeling position, I do draw the line at lounging full length all over the floor. Sometimes we begin with a hymn, as the piano is handy in the livingroom. We usually go around the circle and ask for any petitions. Then we say a memorized prayer familiar to everyone and ask if anyone wants to pray spontaneously. We conclude with a prayer by my husband or myself asking God's special blessing on each of us in turn. The words of this prayer depend on what is currently going on in everyone's life. For example, Chris

44

may have to deal with a best friend moving away. Noelle is starting high school next week. She will need special grace to get off to a good start. Jay is beginning a new job. Beth is traveling far away in Europe. We pray for her safety. Rob and his wife Melissa are making the long trip from Colorado to our house by car. And so it goes. We lift each of our children up to God in prayer, asking whatever blessings each one needs.

The youngest gets to blow out the candle. As soon as the last "Amen" was said there used to be a stampede for the candle. Now they know only one of them is the designated candle snuffer.

Sometimes it is easier to fit family prayer into a block of time which is already scheduled for something. I always found it convenient to have family prayers immediately after dinner. It makes more sense to keep people together who were already congregated in one place than to have to go around gathering them all up again.

Your children need to know when this prayer time is scheduled as well as when and how long they are expected to be present. We have family prayer once a week for about ten minutes. If we intend to have a more elaborate evening of family prayers we let them know in advance. The more you communicate your plans all around the less chance for unpleasant surprises.

At our house the high school children are expected to set aside at least an hour for homework each school night, with time left over for showers and snacks. The grade school children set aside half an hour, with their baths coming right after homework time. Usually all this begins about 7:00, and it is no hardship to plan dinner a little earlier one evening a week and have family prayers at 6:30 or from 6:45 to 7:15 if extra time is needed for a longer session. We are flexible both in setting the time for prayers to begin and in determining their duration.

You may be one of the lucky few who does not need to schedule your evenings quite so tightly. It may be just as easy for your family, especially if there are fewer of you, to pray together for a while before dinner or later in the evening.

There's nothing magic about evenings either. Any time of the day that is convenient for your family is good for prayer. If your children are very young and your partner is available, afternoons are lovely. Most pre-schoolers take a nap during the day. Set your prayer time right before the children's naps. Instead of the livingroom, pray together in their room or in your bedroom. Whatever works for you and feels right for the family is your obvious choice.

The important thing is to stress a definite date and time each week. Otherwise, days and evenings tend to be nibbled away by television, phone calls and the general busy-ness of living.

Setting aside ten or fifteen minutes daily or weekly is not likely to disturb anyone's schedule. If you plan to gather for a longer and more elaborate family prayer time this will require a close scrutiny of television listings and practice schedules if your children are highly involved in sports or other structured activities such as lessons and scouts. Remember how you avoided mutiny and tears when you wisely scheduled your Bible reading around favorite shows (Chapter Two)? Do the same now with family prayer evenings. You will fare better by accomodating your schedule to the Disney movie than by belligerently insisting that prayer time is more important and, "We are going to do this on Monday night, yes Monday night and I don't care what is on television." The same reasoning applies to cub scouts and soccer practice. It does seem ludicrous that the TV guide can control our free time to that extent, but modern living being what it is, we all make compromises.

What do I mean by a more elaborate prayer gathering? In our family, once a month or bi-monthly we gather everyone together for half an hour or so in the evening. We begin as usual with candle lighting and a song around the piano. Then, using the familiar prayers that all of us have heard and said in church since we were very young, we look very carefully at one prayer, think about it, and realize what we are communicating when we say that prayer.

One ready example is the Lord's Prayer. Sometime before

we meet I jot down some notes and include selected Scripture passages. My notes may look something like this:

Introduction:
1. The story of how Jesus introduced the Lord's prayer ... Read Luke 11:1-4 aloud.
2. Discuss the address and petitions one by one.

Address:
"OUR FATHER WHO ART IN HEAVEN...." Call God by name. Why can we do this?

Petitions:
1. "HALLOWED BE THY NAME...." His name should be hallowed and praised. Is it? Why not?
2. "THY KINGDOM COME, THY WILL BE DONE ON EARTH AS IT IS IN HEAVEN...." These two petitions pertain to spiritual things.
3. "GIVE US THIS DAY OUR DAILY BREAD...." This pertains to earthly needs.
4. "AND FORGIVE US OUR TRESPASSES AS WE FOR-GIVE THOSE WHO TRESPASS AGAINST US...." A dangerous petition. What are we saying to God? Should He take us at our word and really do unto us as we do unto others? Good discussion point with the children.
5. "AND LEAD US NOT INTO TEMPTATION...." Can we interpret this as giving us strength to resist temptation?
6. "BUT DELIVER US FROM EVIL. AMEN." What is evil? Does it ever look inviting?

At the end of the session we all say the Lord's Prayer together. There is no end to prayers that can be shared this way. The Psalms are beautiful prayers, although with the exception of the twenty-third psalm, they are not as familiar to most people as the prayers we are used to hearing in church.

If this seems like too much work, pick up a book on family prayers. Most of these books center prayers around different spiritual themes and take you through a complete family prayer. It's all there in black and white. (see Resources)

Children — Young and Old

If your children are under eight be thankful you started family prayers so early in their lives. They are not likely to drag their feet when you suggest praying together. Take care to keep your prayer times short and as much on their level as possible. It's the older children who may give you a rough time.

Don't expect a standing ovation when you announce that the family will be setting aside some time to pray together. Include them in your plans, of course, but make it clear that this is an adult decision.

Very young children often believe that God lives in church. In admonishing them over and over each Sunday to be still and be quiet because "we are in God's house," we give them the impression that this pretty flower-filled place called church is where God the Father lives with Jesus along with the Holy Spirit who flies around in there too. Once a week we get dressed up and visit them. At an early age we need to bring God out of His church and into our homes and into our lives. Family prayers are a step in this direction.

When children are very young, and before their enthusiasm is chipped away by various societal ills, they are completely open (as opposed to being self-conscious) at prayer. They will gladly pray aloud spontaneously in front of anyone. You can teach them short memorized prayers or pray with them in friendly conversation with their God.

Being naturally curious, they will listen to your stories about Jesus and about God quite willingly and will ask for more long after you are ready to go on to something else. Spending time with you, their most important person, holds their attention. Take advantage of this short and very precious time. It will not come again. All too soon they will be clamoring for the car keys and a new prom dress.

Older children and teenagers are something all together different. If you insist that everyone in the family be present for prayer time you may get some sullen company for a while. I felt that the physical presence of our teens and pre-teens set an example for their younger siblings. My husband was all for going ahead without them. We finally did insist that anyone

48

under eighteen must join the family for prayers. As time went by and family prayers became an institution in our lives, the older children abandoned their bored poses and began to participate freely.

Face it, you cannot force another person to pray. Mumbling words is not necessarily communication with God. When our older children did not feel compelled to involve themselves in prayer, they were asked to sit quietly while the rest of us continued.

There may come a time when your older children confess that they no longer believe in prayer in any form. They may even tell you outright that praying is a silly waste of time and "Who listens anyway?" It is best at this point to back off and do nothing for a while. What can be done, after all? Prayer is a private matter. You cannot very well lock the reluctant children in their rooms and yell through the door, "Now pray, already!"

If your relationship is open enough you might try to talk to them about what prayer means in your life. This neatly takes the children out of the spotlight but leaves the subject open. You might bring them some books to read. Sometimes such an intellectual and objective approach is viewed as a challenge rather than a personal affront.

For better or for worse, it is true that our children tend to be more impacted by what we *do* in our lives than what we *say*. If our lives are a prayer, as they should be, if our children see us giving our time, our attention and our respect to them and to others, they are more likely to believe what we say about living in God's kingdom.

The important thing here is not to allow the subject of family prayer to become overblown and develop into a chasm which pulls you out of reach of each other.

You can, and I believe you should, include them in family prayers, Scripture reading, grace at meals and whatever the rest of the family does along this line. It does no one any good to foster a spiritual drop-out. And all the while you can continue to pray *for* them. Always.

Other considerations

Time and setting are not the only ingredients in a plan for family prayer time. Each person living in your house is an individual with a personal idea of God and of prayer. These individuals who make up your family must first be comfortable with God alone before they can talk with Him and praise Him publicly. If your family members have been in the habit of attending church and Sunday school, saying private prayers and some form of family prayer like grace at meals, you have very little groundwork to lay.

If your family is only marginally aware of God and of prayer, the groundwork has to be laid before family prayer can proceed with any degree of success.

Were I in the latter situation, I would probably begin by having the family attend church regularly. The music, the sermon, the prayers and, of course, Sunday school all help to familiarize the family with God. If my spouse was willing and my children mature enough, I might give them some books on prayer. Slowly, as the family began to feel more comfortable with God, I would introduce grace at meals, family Scripture reading and family prayers. All of this takes time and great patience.

Odd as it may seem, one of the obstacles that gets in the way of good family prayer time might be our own unbridled enthusiasm and zealous efforts to teach. Be aware that these times of family prayer are not mini-lessons. You are not their religion instructor, making up lesson plans and worrying about what and how much they have learned.

Certainly we all expect to gain some insights, some spiritual growth from this experience, but keep the primary purpose in mind: We are praying together, sharing a communication with our God and with each other. We are bringing God into our homes and into our lives through prayer.

Teaching Scripture and church doctrine surely has its place. Combining that kind of teaching with prayer, though, is a mistake. Even the longer prayer times, when we delve into a single prayer together, are not meant to be lessons. The notes I take are only for the purpose of stimulating discussion and helping me remember some important facts.

Another obstacle, at least in the beginning, is a reluctance to pray aloud or share our petitions. Adolescents are especially reticent to share their prayers aloud. They have a horror of "messing up" in public, no matter how insignificant the "mess up" or the public. They may be far more comfortable praying alone in their darkened bedrooms. Sometimes they tend to hide their reticense by clowning or poking fun at a brother or sister who stumbles over a word or cannot think of a petition.

It helps to have a private talk with each child before attempting family prayers. Speak with them frankly, kindly, and most important, privately. Remember, under that smooth bravado lurks a quivering, easily wounded ego.

Time is on your side. If you have kept the atmosphere open and caring, your older children may eventually jump the hurdle of self-consciousness and find themselves praying, singing and discussing along with the rest of the family.

What if they do not, you say? What if they dig in their heels and refuse to ever pray and participate? Don't let it throw you. Whatever you do, don't let their attitude stop the rest of the family from praying together. Pray for them. Pray for yourself, for patience and wisdom to handle them with love. You have done all you can by bringing family prayer into your home, by encouraging them and by setting certain standards of behavior and respect for prayer.

Thank God for your beautiful children and then leave them to Him. Recall the words of Paul: "Be joyful and pray at all times, be thankful in all circumstances. This is what God wants from you and your life in union with Christ Jesus" (Thessalonians 5:16-18).

Holidays Are Holy Days

Today's families. How different they are from the families I grew up with. Children are shuttled off to play centers, child care centers, pre-schools and play schools almost as soon as they can toddle.

Old people cluster in retirement communities. Young parents struggle to hold down several jobs. Older parents worry over college tuition, SAT scores and keeping the kids off drugs and alcohol. Nobody has time to talk with anyone else, let alone listen with compassion. Rarely does the family sit down all together to a quiet meal without someone having to jump up and rush off to ball practice or scouts or a meeting.

Who are all these strangers living under one roof?

How have we allowed our lives to get so out of control that we buzz through activities at top speed? Worst of all, each of us may be buzzing in a different direction, barely making contact with each other as we go.

Family Scripture reading and family prayer are two ways to regulate the harried pace and govern more closely the influence and pressures of the world outside your door. By the very nature of what you must do to accomplish these family times (limit television, schedule time together, share and cooperate), you begin to regulate time and commitments within your home.

Holiday rituals are another way to bring spiritual refreshment to your family. Picture a Christmas morning when the children do not tear open package after package, only to ask, "Is that all?" Picture a Lent crowned with the Lord's Last Supper at your own family table. Consider Halloween week as more than just costumes and candy, but a time when we remember our own dead.

From ritual grows unity. If your family can begin to see God's hand in the holidays, the seasonal changes of the year, the secular rush and bustle that accompanies our major holidays will become less important.

The two great feasts of Christmas and Easter furnish the focal points for these rituals, although other lesser occasions can be celebrated in your family (as they are in ours). Our home rituals were planned and developed over the years and incorporated into our family's spiritual life a little at a time. You may want to add, delete and make changes to fit your own household.

Begin, as always, by talking with your spouse or adult partner. Since these rituals do change the manner of celebrating the big holidays, you may want to talk with your older children as well, before going ahead with major alterations.

Lent
Unlike the merry feast of Christmas, our first extended home ritual of the year is a somber occasion. Reflecting on the

cross, the death and the resurrection of Christ brings a quieter joy than the celebration of Jesus' birth. Luckily, Easter has not been as grossly commercialized as Christmas. So much the better, for now you can make this season exactly what you want it to be. You and your partner can determine how Easter is to be celebrated with minimal interference from the Easter Bunny.

Talk with your partner. Recall Lent and Easter from past years. How would you like to make this year different? What would you like to see your family gain from your walk through Lent?

Are you facing Lent as a single parent this year? Since the Easter feast tends to bring far-flung relatives together at a holiday table, you may want to search out a brother or sister, preferably with children, to join you in your Lenten preparations and rituals. If that is not possible perhaps a friend with children close in age to your own may want to partner with you and provide a good Lent for both families. Follow a sensible plan for getting together with these people outside your immediate family (see Chapter One).

Lenten preparations usually require a combination of prayers, good works and meditation, some on a daily basis, some weekly. Your bookstore and library will yield a host of books to choose from that will take you through the days of Lent with a great variety of prayers, readings and activities. Since your Lenten preparation is a daily experience, you will need even more cooperation from the family than for Scripture reading or family prayer which can be spaced out over weeks and months.

Together with your spouse or partner, look at the complexity of your days with a realistic eye. How much time can you spare each day? Even if you add a small Lenten prayer to every dinner grace, that is something more than you have done in previous years. Do not try to take it all in the first year: prayers, readings and special liturgies. It would be gratifying to meditate daily and call the family together each evening for prayer and Scripture, and show the children by your example what good works should be. But is all this

54

feasible? Probably not. Certainly not that first fledgling year or two when you are introducing family prayer and feeling like a novice. Limit your plans to what you can realistically accomplish.

The beginning of Lent is a little like the beginning of summer vacation. Remember that first fresh breath of summer freedom when we plan far more than can be fulfilled in one short season? Time looks limitless with long green-and-gold days going on and on. So it is with Lent. The days till Easter stretch ahead and we feel that almost anything is possible. Not so. If you look at your lifestyle realistically you will admit, I'm sure, that your actual free time is quite limited. While preparing for guests, traveling to visit the relatives, getting a decent outfit assembled for each of your children and winding things up at work before the holiday, the days will fly by. Realistically, there isn't a great deal of time for prayer, Scripture and family rituals.

Having achieved some semblance of harmony between your schedule and your plans for Lent, you should be aware of another potential stumbling block: the people outside your immediate family, your relatives and parents, those dear ones without whom a big holiday like Easter seems incomplete. I think most of us are still affected by the Currier and Ives syndrome, no matter how streamlined and modernized our living.

Easter evokes a picture of a diningroom papered in chintz with extra chairs drawn up to a large table and relatives in their new finery gathered around.

Never mind the fact that most grandmothers these days are dedicated to diets and aerobics, and have exchanged their aprons for two-piece suits and, in some cases, jeans. Grandfathers are busy shining up the mobile campers and studying road maps against that long-planned cross-country trip. You can't get away from it: even today family ties are strongest at holiday time and the bigger the holiday, the more nostalgia there is drifting through the air.

If there is a traditional gathering of the clan at Easter time how will you handle your Lenten preparations, prayers and rituals? Good hearted and loving as these folks may be, they could look upon your Lent as an affront to what they consider proper or, worse than this, superfluous. Plowing through all these new plans for the first time with your own family is arduous enough. What you do not need right now is anyone undermining your plans or goals.

Be especially careful if you are a single parent, newly widowed or divorced. With the best of intentions, even your distant relatives may see it as their role to guide you, and blueprint your life on all fronts. Very young, newly married couples may also be subjected to this kind of benign manipulation.

Once you and your spouse or partner have decided to go ahead with your Lenten prayers, make that a priority and work the relatives in around your plans. If, for example, you always drive a long distance to spend Easter with the grandparents, plan to complete your prayers and special rituals (like the Sedar meal) before leaving home.

If the relatives gather at your house for Easter, offer to include them in a simple Lenten prayer service, but don't plan to include a lot of visitors in something as complicated as the Sedar meal unless they are very interested in participating.

Suppose you have relatives who live far away and will be coming to spend the week before Easter with you. Now you have not only dinner guests, but houseguests who must be fed and entertained and made to feel at home. Welcome as such a visit may be, it complicates your Lenten renewal. Sedar, the Passover meal which involves a long ritual of prayers and singing at table with the family, should be planned no earlier than the week before Easter, and ideally on Thursday of that week. How can you celebrate a Sedar meal in the middle of a bunch of relatives who are, at best, uninterested and perhaps, even hostile to the idea?

One way to do this is to make your noon meal the Sedar meal. If work schedules at your house prevent you from doing this on Thursday, try Saturday this year. First explain your plans to your guests, with as much or as little embellishment as you need. Then suggest that they have lunch comfortably (in front of the television, if possible) in a room far enough removed from where the Sedar meal will be served to allow both groups privacy. When you are ready to begin the Sedar ritual, enlist the help of your family in serving sandwiches and tea or chili and beer, or whatever seems best and easiest, to your guests. Once your houseguests are settled and fed, your family can begin the Sedar meal. Go through the prayers and the responses and the singing right up to the point where you would bring the meal to the table at the end of the ritual. Stop here and instead of eating apart from your company, join them at this point, wherever they are and share their lunch.

Granted, this is not the best atmosphere to enjoy your Sedar ritual, and it is doubly difficult if you have small children or small visitors. Either your own will want to stay and watch television with the cousins, or the cousins will be enormously curious about what you are doing at the table. Either way, some of the fun and unity of the ritual will be lost. If your family is committed to a Sedar meal each Lent, it is up to you and your spouse to arrange visits in such a way as to keep these disruptions to a minimum.

Handle all this casually, calmly, without fuss and with no apologies. Eventually your relatives will catch on to the fact that this is your home, your children, your customs and rituals. They may not like it, but they will accept it.

Do not apologize for or disguise any of your rituals or Lenten preparations. If you keep an "alms jar," as we do, on the kitchen counter and your aunt becomes distinctly curious, explain that it is used to hold the sacrificial giving of all the family, and at the end of Lent the accumulated monies will go to the soup kitchen. She may sniff at this and give you a lecture on sustaining people who refuse to sustain themselves. Listen with sweet patience and continue to urge your family to drop quarters, dollars and dimes into the jar. Do not give in to temptation and hide the jar before your aunt arrives.

In other words, know what you want to do, plan it with your spouse, then carry it out. Period. If your relatives want to participate, fine. If not, carry out most of your plans in their absence, if that seems feasible.

Suppose you or one of your family members has written an Easter grace which you plan to use before the big feast. Also suppose that in your extended family grace is not a habit. A large and jolly crowd has gathered at your house for Easter dinner. You are nervously helping your spouse get it on the table, wondering all the while how you will stop all those people from beginning to eat before you've had a chance to thank God in prayer. There is no reason to abandon table prayer on this most holy day of the year. Nor is there a need to coach the company ahead of time.

Call the company to dinner with everything set and prepared, but leave the food out in the kitchen. Once you are all seated say something like, "Beth will you read the prayer you wrote for Easter?" or "Let's bow our heads for a minute." Then one of you can say a prayer or read from Scripture or whatever you had planned. You might even ask your company to hold hands around the table. That's all. Don't force anyone who has not been in on the planning of these Lenten preparations from the beginning to sit through a long, elaborate ritual.

If you are serving a buffet instead of a sit-down dinner, call everyone around the buffet table while you stand directly in front of the pile of plates and silverware. No one can start in on the food while you are obstructing their access to the plates. Then go ahead with grace and afterward move away from the plates, allowing people to get to the food.

What about Easter dinner at someone else's house? In your own home you and your spouse set the rules as well as the spiritual atmosphere. Obviously the same is true in the homes of your relatives and friends. It would be as boorish to insist on following your religious rituals in another's home as it would be for anyone to make a mockery of what you do in yours.

Sedar: The Last Supper
From our Jewish friends we have borrowed the ritual of the Sedar meal, the Passover meal, the Lord's Last Supper, and have made it our own. The word Passover means "deliverance." In the book of Exodus, God passed over the

houses of the children of Israel and delivered them from their oppressors (Ex. 12:27). The Passover feast in the Jewish tradition is a seven day festival and centers on a special meal: the Sedar meal. This meal commemorates the events of Exodus and is rich with songs, prayers, commentary, and the general merriment of a group of people rejoicing and praising their God.

On the night He was betrayed, Jesus sat with His disciples at a meal much like the one we put on our table. That meal, known to Christians the world over as the Last Supper, was a Sedar meal celebrating the Passover.

Everything about the Sedar meal appealed to me when I first witnessed it in the home of a friend. With some minor changes we adapted it to our family table, and now each Lent is crowned with the gathering of whichever children and children-in-law happen to be home for Easter week.

The primary aim of the Sedar meal is to pass on to the next generation the story of our spiritual heritage and the deliverance by Yahweh of His people. It is by no means a solemn fold-your-hands-and-bow-your-heads occasion. When our family was younger the Sedar meal was fraught with as many dining disasters as any other meal at our house. The baby fussed. Toddlers spilled milk into their shoes, and my husband presided over all this with the pained expression of a man who had been thrust into a role for which he has had no preparation. As the family grew and the years turned unfailingly in their cycle from Lent to Easter to Thanksgiving to Advent to Christmas and back to Lent again, our Sedar celebrations began to smooth out and take on the look of a true family tradition. Everyone knew his or her part in the prayers and commentaries. The recipes were old hat now and the Bible verses familiar.

We evolved our Sedar ritual using a combination of several sources with some additions of our own. If you decide to incorporate this as part of your Lenten tradition, be aware that it does involve considerable work, especially the first few times you go through it when everything is unfamiliar.

This is one ritual that got the complete nod from every

member of the family. It is, after all, a joyous celebration, coming at the close of a solemn season of fasting and prayer. Although not exactly a feast, it is a meal that brings together several interesting and delightful elements: wine, lamb, the sweetness of haroset, the unusual taste and texture of matzah and the bitterness of the maror. A large meal during Lent would not be in keeping with our preparations and fasting. Instead, we take an evening out to remember our spiritual heritage and taste some unfamiliar foods, sing some songs and pray. Each person at table has an active role to play as the story of Exodus unfolds.

Schedule for a Sedar Meal

Everyone participating in this meal will need a copy of the ritual. It might be a good idea to make copies for all the children who have graduated out of high chairs, even those who cannot read. Just handling the papers and trying to follow along makes some children feel a part of the ritual. On the other hand, I've had several who get terribly frustrated if they cannot follow every word, and soon papers get shuffled into a messy little mound and tears flow. You will know best how to include your younger ones without frustrating them.

Several days or even weeks before the scheduled Sedar, which should be held, if at all possible, on the last Thursday before Easter, you will want to gather some songs to sing together. Most families have taken a turn at singing Christmas carols at one time or another. Singing around the table at a meal is a little unusual but is no more difficult than gathering around the piano or under a snowy lampost for caroling. We happen to have several musicians in the family, so my youngest daughter Noelle and I spend some time at the piano looking over music and trying out the hymns. If you are unfamiliar with the names of hymns but remember a few from church services that appeal to you, you might contact your pastor or choir leader for names or recommendations of songs. If your family shuns music you could forget about the singing, but in doing so you will lose much of the richness of this ritual.

After selecting the songs I play them on our piano and record them on tape. This takes the place of accompaniment when we sing together at the table, as the piano is located in the livingroom and we eat our Sedar meal in the diningroom. If you play the guitar or small keyboard, that would be a good way to keep everyone on key, and it is much easier than fussing with a tape recorder during the meal.

Prepare the *haroset* on the evening before the Sedar meal. It is more flavorful after spending the night blending in the refrigerator:

> 1 cup chopped nuts (do not grind)
> 1 cup chopped apples
> 1 T cinnamon
> 1/4 cup honey
> 1/2 cup raisins
> Red wine if desired

Combine well and refrigerate overnight. Vary the proportions according to your family's taste. If your family has a sweet tooth and you do not make haroset during the year, you will find that they look forward to this annual Sedar meal treat.

Maror is a bitter herb. You can use horseradish root, ground horseradish right from the jar or parsley.

Eggs are symbolic of new life and this meal requires each person to have a slice of hard boiled egg.

Wine should be red, not white and should be sufficient for each person to have one glass. Grape juice is a good substitute for children and those adults who do not care for wine. Try to find a delicious sparkling grape juice which would be a little more festive than the plain variety.

Matzoh can be found in most grocery stores around the time of Easter. If you cannot find it make your own:

> 3 1/4 cups flour
> 1 cup water
> 1 T salt

Mix all ingredients well. Divide into three equal balls of dough. Shape each into a very thin circle 6 to 8 inches in diameter. Place on a greased cookie sheet and prick the dough with a fork. Bake at 500 for 5-6 minutes or until brown.

A separate small dish of salt water should be placed next to each person's plate. A napkin should be placed on a separate plate. This will be used during the meal to cover the "hidden portion" or the *afikoman.*

You will need some representation of the paschal lamb. I usually save the bone of lamb we grill in summer and store it in the freezer.

The table can be set early that day or even the day before. Use your good table settings: china, glassware, silver, linens. Bring the festive touch to your table with flowers, candles or other pretty accessories. We have two intricate brass birds that rested in the middle of our table among the candles when our children were small enough to worry about breakage of more delicate items. Nothing could harm those birds and they added a touch of elegance in the candlelight even though none of the china matched and the children used plastic glasses.

Everyone will need some kind of glass for wine and another for water. Fill the water glasses in advance if you like but the wine glasses should remain empty before the meal.

Put out a basket of Matzoh. Place the lamb bone somewhere near whomever will be the leader in your ritual. Everything that will be used in the Sedar ritual should be on the table before the family sits down. Keep the actual meal out in the kitchen to be eaten when the prayers, songs and commentaries are finished. We usually have a hearty chicken soup and a casserole, two things that can be kept warm for a long time without harm. This keeps things simple. We are, after all, still in the season of Lent and a large sumptuous meal would be out of place.

When people come to the Sedar table they should each find on their plate:

> a slice of hard boiled egg
> a bitter herb
> a piece of matzoh
> a small dish with salt water (shot glasses are good, also
> egg cups)

I use small dessert plates for all this and later bring in the dinner plates and soup bowls for the remainder of the meal.

You will want to decide well ahead of time which adult will be the leader. If you are lucky enough to have a grandparent who is enthusiastic about this it would be meaningful for that person, as the oldest family member, to preside. If your children are old enough to read they too have roles to play in the Sedar meal. Certainly, it would do no harm to go over their parts a few days before the meal. Although there is no memorization involved, you would be wise to talk with them about what you are doing and what role each person plays as the youngest, middle or oldest child. When we first brought the Sedar to our house we made sure that every literate child had something to read.

In adapting the ritual Sedar meal to our family's Lenten preparation, I used two books almost exclusively: *Christ In The Passover* by Ceil and Moishe Rosen and *Family Lenten Handbook: Change My Heart* published by Paulist Press. Since we brought the Sedar celebration into our home years ago, I have noticed many of the newer Lenten handbooks are including it as part of Lenten renewal. If you are interested in this celebration you should have no problem finding material to assist you.

Advent

Advent is derived from the word *adventus*, which means "coming." Christians throughout the world prepare for the coming of the Christ child in special ways. For years we had given token recognition to Advent by lighting a candle each Sunday in the Advent wreath and saying a prayer. Somewhere along the way this no longer seemed to satisfy us as a suitable preparation of the heart and mind to welcome the Christ child on Christmas.

At a Bible study class I was introduced to the Jesse Tree prayers. I brought them home and we have used this ritual, along with the Advent wreath, ever since to complete our spiritual preparation for celebrating the birthday of Christ.

Jesus was a descendant of the "house of David." Joseph, the earthly father of Jesus, and husband of Mary, was a member

63

of the family of David. David was the son of Jesse. Through the Jesse Tree prayers we trace the earthly family lineage of Jesus. The readings for this ritual are taken from both the Old and the New Testaments. There is a reading and a prayer for each day of December that focuses on the coming of Jesus and on His family history.

The Jesse Tree Symbols

Since the Jesse Tree prayers begin the first day of December, you must have the symbols ready and completed by November 30. You will need twenty-seven symbols cut from balsa wood or felt and decorated. Unless you want to end this ritual on Christmas Day, in which case you will need only twenty-five. The daily ritual begins with a Scripture reading, then goes on to an explanation of the symbol for that reading. A prayer follows and, last of all, the symbol is hung on the Jesse Tree. By Christmas Eve twenty-four symbols bedeck the little tree and add a festive touch to the house, as well as a reminder of the family's continued faithful preparations for the climax of this holy season.

Once you have made the twenty-seven symbols your work is complete. They last for years with only a bit of retouching now and then. The only thing left for you to do is remember where you stashed them for safekeeping from one December to the next.

We made ours of heavy white felt with gold glitter. One bleak Sunday in November, I called the children around the kitchen table which was loaded with white felt, glue, scissors, pencils and gold glitter. I talked to them about the story of King David that we had already read in one of our family Scripture sessions. We talked about David's father Jesse and about Joseph, the father of Jesus, who was descended from "the house of David." We also talked about family trees. Robbie had made a family tree in school that year which was hanging in his room. We brought it down and traced the branches that represented his grandparents, cousins, aunts, and uncles. This helped put the Jesse Tree into perspective.

Then we got busy (all of us, including my husband and

myself) making the symbols for the Jesse Tree. You know by now that I would have had a talk with my husband before going ahead with all this. Get an early start if you want the Jesse Tree to become part of your family's Advent preparation. Once you and your spouse or adult partner agree to do this you need to plan a time when the whole family can become involved with the preparations. This is most important. It may be easier for you to sit down in front of the television some evening to cut out and decorate the symbols yourself. I'm sure they would be lovely. An angel drawn by an adult tends to resemble a credible angel far more than one rendered by a four-year old's unsteady hand. Our angel for the Jesse Tree was made by Jay when he was six. It is a white felt effigy with bald head and two huge, heavy-lidded eyes. The smile is Cheshire, the wings two tiny stumps. All this is generously embellished with gold glitter. A stranger seeing this angel flying on our Jesse Tree might cringe, but we all remember the night he made it and how proud he was of his creation. We remember the laughter around the table, the sticky fingers and the cats licking glitter out of their fur.

Be aware that if you pass up this opportunity to create your Jesse Tree symbols together you may be overlooking a symbol of another kind. There is no better way to interest children in a ritual and make it their own than to involve them in the hands-on preparations for that ritual. Involving yourself in these preparations gives them an added importance in your children's eyes.

Assemble all your materials on an evening when you can be fairly sure everyone will be home, and no one will bemoan the loss of a favorite television show. Talk with the children about family history and family trees. Depending on the ages of the children and your own preference, tell the story of David and his father Jesse or read it from Scripture (I Samuel 16).

Explain that this year, starting with the first day of December, you will gather each day to say a prayer and read Scripture to learn more about the family tree of Jesus and to get ready for His birthday.

As with any project that involves several young children

and is apt to create mess as well as artistry, plan for the safety of your floors and table. If your kitchen has a carpeted floor, covering the space under the table with an old shower curtain or plastic drop cloth helps to keep glue out of your carpet. Cover the table top with oilcloth or plastic and space the children so that you or your spouse are handy to help small fingers with scissors and glitter.

Look over your copy of the Jesse Tree prayers and write down the symbols on individual pieces of paper. These papers will then be folded and dropped into a pot. Each person chooses one folded paper as the pot is passed around until all the papers are gone. These are the assigned symbols for which each person will be responsible. This method seems to be not only fair but also quick and as free of argument as any project involving young children. If your children are in their teens and you find it easier to have each person choose several symbols, fine. You know best what works with your family.

Once the symbols are ready you will need to find an appropriate "tree" to be your Jesse Tree. We use a large houseplant that resembles a palm tree. A Norfolk pine or an orange tree make a good base for the Jesse Tree symbols. If you are worried about possible damage to your houseplants, buy a small artificial desk tree which should last forever.

Since the Jesse Tree ritual requires daily prayers you must find the least disruptive time when most of the family will be home. With our older family, we have found the time immediately before dinner to be best. When the children were much younger and spent their evenings at home, we would recite the Jesse Tree prayers right before homework time. Because no one was allowed out on school nights and homework time began promptly at 7:00, it was easy to fit the Jesse Tree prayers into that slot. Like most good intentions, this ritual will fall by the wayside unless you set a time at the very beginning and stick to it. The whole thing takes ten minutes at the most, but those ten minutes can and will get eaten up by odds and ends of everyone's evening unless given the same importance as any other appointment.

Christmas Eve

If there is a night more beautiful, suspenseful, nerve-wracking, spiritual, tense and gratifying than Christmas Eve, I don't know of it. For years my husband and I struggled to shape this one special night and the next day into some semblance of what we felt it should be. Valiantly we fought the battle of the "gimmies" and the "grabbies," the high pitched wrangling of tired, overstimulated little children who wanted to stay up to see Santa, the Man of the Hour. Year after year we vowed to set a better spiritual tone for our Christmas Eve and, finally, we did.

If your house holds several Santa-believers you may have noticed that the pre-Christmas push by the toy industry seems to start grabbing at these children earlier each year. We may yet live to see kids making out their Christmas lists in the hot dog days of August.

We begin our preparation for a spiritual Christmas Eve the week before Christmas by cutting back on the television watching. We bring home good VCR tapes with a Christmas theme (Santa included) and use these as a substitute for some of the commercial laden tripe that passes for children's seasonal entertainment.

If you have not invested in a VCR you might want to read aloud to your younger ones from some of the special Christmas stories you can find on any library shelf. If yours are pre-school age take some holiday records or tapes out of the public library. These are entertaining, good for jumping and dancing and, best of all, free of toy commercials.

Why do all this the week before Christmas when you are at your busiest? Because if you do not take steps to start winding down the hectic pace and commercial push for your children *before* Christmas Eve, the nervous energy will surely find its final outlet on that evening. Trying to interest them in the real Christmas story and quiet prayer will have the same success as stopping a merry-go-round with a grab of your hand.

Plan your shopping, wrapping, card sending, and especially toy assembling so as to leave Christmas Eve open as much as possible. Plan your big meal for the afternoon. This frees you from cooking and washing dishes later in the evening. In our family the older children (teens and college students) are asked to stay home that one night in the year, at least until our ritual is complete and the little ones are off to bed. You may have trouble with this if your older children are used to going out on Christmas Eve. Whatever you do, do not spring it on them December 23rd. Talk with them sometime before mid-December and enlist their cooperation in staying home with the family for at least part of the evening. If this creates a real wrangle, let it go. You are better off having your Christmas Eve ritual without them than risking an atmosphere charged with mutiny and bad feelings. I am talking now about sons and daughters who are of late high school and college age, not the thirteen to fifteen-year olds who should still expect to follow parental suggestions.

Sometime after the dinner mess is cleared up and your younger ones have had their baths, gather everyone in the livingroom. Make this as early as possible. It might help to remind your true believers that early bedtime on Christmas Eve brings Santa's visit that much sooner, as it is a well known fact that he never arrives while children are awake. If your family likes singing together, sing some carols around the piano or a keyboard. If they balk at singing, put carols on the record player and listen together, admire the tree, wind down the pace of this past week. If your younger ones have a special pillow or blanket that makes them feel snug and secure, by all means bring it down. Light the candles and the fireplace, if you have one. Everyone should feel warm and comfortable and cozy. This is the atmosphere you want to create. Bring the Bible and have someone read aloud the Christmas story from Luke. Go over the verses well ahead of time and choose those which should be read. Very young children will squirm and itch if the reading lasts too long, and Luke's second chapter contains 52 verses.

If your Christmas tradition includes an annual readingof *The Night Before Christmas* or Dickens' *Christmas Carol*, save those for bedtime stories after your Bible reading. When you have completed reading whatever verses from Luke you decided to read, ask someone to say a short prayer asking God to bless everyone in the house this special night and whatever else you want to include. We include petitions in our Christmas Eve prayer, especially for the poor and hungry.

Now is the time for hot chocolate, cookies or other refreshments. Unless your children are older, it is not a good idea to bring out spillable refreshments while you are reading from Scripture. Small children tend to become absorbed in the story and dribble hot chocolate or milk on each other. This will cause considerable commotion and disrupt the story. After their bedtime snack little ones can put out something for Santa, hang their stockings, and then run upstairs for prayers and bed. If you manage all this as early as possible, you will still have much of the evening left for final preparations for tomorrow and some time to relax and consider the significance of the feast you are celebrating.

Like Easter and Thanksgiving, the Christmas holidays bring families together, for a day, several days or even several weeks. If you are hosting the family this year and they are at your house on Christmas Eve, how will you manage the extra cooking, sleeping accommodations and stress that a houseful of company always provides along with your Christmas Eve ritual? First of all, be prepared for some criticism from the relatives, especially if this is your first try for a special and spiritual Christmas Eve. When young children are involved, grandparents, aunts and uncles sometimes tend to overreact to any changes in the routine. All of us have memories of our own childhood Christmases, some beautiful and some not so good. We relive our fondest memories in the lives of our children and grandchildren, sometimes not even realizing that we do so. It is quite natural for grandparents to insist that your Christmas Eve traditions continue as always, without additions or deletions. This is important to them. Santa Claus is such fun for grandparents and doting aunts and uncles. Explain as gently as possible that you will not be taking away any of the treasured old rituals, but instead will be making room for some new ones. Whatever you have allowed before (unless it is something you have rethought and decided is not good), continue to allow for the children. The singing and Scripture reading and praying during a quiet time before bed is an important part of Christmas Eve and will only enhance the secular celebration.

Disruption of your ritual, sarcasm about what you are attempting to do or arguments in front of your impressionable children — must not be allowed. Explain your position clearly and with no apologies. It will be accepted after a time, believe me. Perhaps those relatives who are in total disagreement with what you are doing will simply stay away for a while on Christmas Eve, and perhaps that is best.

When you spend Christmas Eve at someone else's house do not expect to dictate the atmosphere or rituals there. If you want a quiet, spiritual Christmas Eve, plan to stay home, at least for the latter part of the day. If your relatives live close enough, you might spend part of the day there and come home to celebrate your own prayer service in the early evening. However you handle this, be aware of other people's needs and emotions as well as their ideas of what Christmas is all about. These may be quite different from yours and from what you want to instill in your children.

You may not be able to have Christmas Eve at home every year, but unless you make some kind of attempt to start your own home rituals and traditions while your children are still young, your own family unit may not grow spiritually. This is something you will need to talk over carefully with your spouse. Whatever you decide about making Christmas Eve rituals reflect the holiness of the season, you must be in agreement. Compromise. Concede here and there. Then, and only then, present a united front to your children, your relatives and other Christmas guests. One more thing: making these home rituals part of your Christmas and Easter traditions takes commitment. Planning and carrying out these rituals has to become as much a priority as the shopping, baking, cooking, entertaining, and all the other activities associated with these holidays.

Ethnic Celebrations

European countries have deep-rooted holiday traditions that originated in a time when villages were small and families depended on each other for everything. The beautiful processions through the towns and villages of sixteenth century Italy celebrating feast days are a memory in the hearts of many Italian-Americans. Unless a family lives in the Italian North End of Boston, or in an equally ethnic Italian neighborhood, it is not practical to include these processions, with their statues of saints and haunting music, as part of their holiday celebration. We can hardly hope to duplicate the processions, the village carnivals and many of the rich and varied ways in which the people of the Old World celebrated holidays.

Some ethnic celebrations are more easily adopted to a variety of settings than others. For instance, the English custom of serving hot cross buns on Good Friday is easier to adopt than the Italian custom of *L'Agonia* where, on Good

Friday, boys carry candles and figures of the Angel of the Tomb through town to the church. There are scores of books describing ethnic traditions for holidays as they were celebrated long ago and may even be celebrated today in the towns and villages of their origins. They make good reading and certainly help tie your children to their heritage, but most of them are not practical as home celebrations.

The ethnic celebrations and traditions described in this chapter, however, can be easily incorporated. Most will require some work and preparation by an adult member of your household. Ethnic dishes, usually, are more elaborate than our American holiday fare. Decide, along with whoever will be sharing the preparation, how much time and energy you can afford to give to these celebrations. Many of them suggest the company of extended family and friends. Inviting people to share a meal is nice. Preparing a beautiful table and elaborate food *can* be nice for those who have the time and enjoy that kind of work.

As you read various books about ethnic holiday celebrations, you will discover two prevalent threads that run through all of them. The first is, even in customs with origins in pagan rites, there is a distinct Christian, spiritual significance. The second is that most ethnic traditions of celebration involve a gathering of family, friends and special people who only occasionally drift in and out of our lives. These traditions come to us from a time when life was slower-paced, and time given to the preparation and enjoyment of family feasts was considered time well spent.

It may not be possible to introduce all the special traditions suggested here in any one year, especially if the Easter celebration at your house has been rather low key in years past. Instead, touch on the less important celebrations in a less important way and allow more time and energy for planning rituals and celebrations of the high points of the Easter season. Sometimes, if we try to embrace each and every detail of a seasonal feast, fatigue and short tempers cause us to lose the glow and spirituality of the feast.

Long will I remember the year I lived in the kitchen for two straight days, preparing the big Russian Easter feast which the family assured me they were looking forward to all year. I prepared mountains of dishes and filled both our refrigerators with scrumptious food. What happened? The house was filled with cluttered corners. The quiet, spiritual traditions we claim as a family were rushed and harried. In trying to hit every detail of the celebration, I found myself barely skimming the surface and not enriching any of it with time, patience and a quiet attitude of attendance. My family ate the food, quarreled over the chores I was too busy to supervise, and found less joy and meaning in the holiday that year than in any I can remember. By the time Easter morning arrived I was too snappish and tired to enjoy my family, and I am sure they could have traded me in without too many qualms.

In bringing Scripture reading, family prayers and spiritual traditions to your family, you have given them the gift of ritual. Now, by sharing the ethnic roots of the holidays, you celebrate as a family and enrich these traditions.

The great feasts of Easter and Christmas stand as the pillars of Christian celebration. We will look at the ways in which these two holidays are celebrated in five countries and what can you do to bring your ethnic traditions home.

Easter in England

Shrove Tuesday, the day before Lent begins, was set aside by the early church as the day for confession of sins. As the old English word for confess was *shrive*, those Christians who made their confessions were *shrove*.

Older Catholics remember the days when we were compelled to give up meat during Lent. Long ago Lent was a time when Christians avoided all forms of food containing fat. Those with English backgrounds have the custom of Pancake Day on Shrove Tuesday. Since fat had to be used up before Lent began, the early English people fried pancakes, fritters and fried cakes (doughnuts) in order to make the most use of the cooking fat that was left in the house.

In our health conscious society, cooking fats are almost

taboo in the kitchen. We use cooking oils throughout Lent just as much (or as little) as we use them during the rest of the year. Still, it might be nice to buy some doughnuts for dessert on Shrove Tuesday or make for dinner that evening a stack of golden pancakes and sausages with sweet syrup. Talk about the background of your English ancestors. It matters little what kind of fried cakes you have. It is the tradition of having the same thing for this one meal every year, the talking together and perhaps a special prayer to start your family off on a meaningful Lent that counts.

When Good Friday comes around, the English people inevitably think of hot cross buns. These are sweet, raisin-filled buns, with a cross made of frosting across their tops. In Chelsea people were said to line up before six o'clock in the morning to get their hot cross buns for Good Friday from the royal bun houses.

Some people believe that hot cross buns are pagan in origin. As a welcoming rite of spring, the Anglo-Saxons ate sweet cakes. The early Roman missionaries tried to break them of this habit, but when they failed, they decided to bless the sweet cakes and frost them with a cross.

No one in our family is English, but we bake hot cross buns for Good Friday and serve them with dinner that evening. Sometimes we talk about their origins in England. Sometimes we talk about the early Christians and the cross as a symbol. And sometimes we just enjoy them as a yearly treat with totally secular conversation at table.

A charming English tradition kept on the last Sunday of Lent is called "Mothering Sunday." It reminds me of our Mother's Day. On this Sunday, children who lived away from home went back to their home towns, to the churches in which they were baptized. They also visited their mothers and brought small gifts of food, usually cakes, as tokens. Not a difficult Lenten tradition to adopt, and one that would be welcomed by all mothers.

Eggs are ingrained in the Easter celebration of almost every country. English children get chocolate eggs beautifully wrapped in fancy paper. Long ago in England messages were written on eggs and sent to friends. Sometimes the messages were kept for years. If your family is English why not make some of these message-bearing eggs at the same time that your are coloring the regular hard boiled eggs for Easter? If you want to save your eggs as keepsakes, blow the insides out of raw eggs and rinse carefully, then dye. If not mishandled, they will last for years.

Egg rolling is an annual event in England. This is an easy ethnic custom to foster. All you need are some eggs, a grassy hill and some enthusiastic rollers. Actually, this custom has a spiritual message. It represents the rolling away of the stone at Christ's tomb on Easter morning.

When you first adopt these ethnic customs, they may seem a little strange, somewhat out of step with our modern way of living. Yet, in observing them year after year, they become part of our lives, part of our ethnic tradition.

Some of these traditions are just nice to follow, whether you associate them with your own ethnic origins or not. We have an egg tree every Easter. Pancakes are on our table on Shrove Tuesday and hot cross buns on Good Friday. Yet, none of us can claim a bit of English, German or French ancestry. It just happens to be the way we enjoy celebrating the Easter season.

My husband's background is Italian; mine is Russian. We brought a rich cultural heritage to our marriage. Wanting our children to enjoy both Russian and Italian holiday traditions, we share the two big Christian feasts. Our Easter celebration is ethnically Russian, while Christmas brings Italian traditions to our house.

Easter in Germany
The German people also like cakes on Shrove Tuesday, but they lean toward rich crullers fried in fat. Again, these are easily found in most bakeries and in the frozen food section of many groceries. You can make your own crullers and fry them in unsaturated vegetable oil. Call the cakes by their German name, *fastnachts*. Tell your family this means "fast night." In keeping the traditions, be they ever so small, we touch our roots and hold our children close to their origins. In this

fast-paced world of sky rockets and jet travel, it is good to have roots to hold us steady.

All animal fats, milk and eggs were forbidden to Christians in the early Roman Empire during Lent. These Christians learned to make a special dough of salt, flour and water. This they shaped into the form of two crossed arms in an attitude of prayer to remind them of the holiness of Lent. They called these little breads *bracalle* or "little arms." Later the Germans called them *brezel* or *prezel*, and so evolved our pretzels. Pretzels are still a Lenten food in Germany. You can make simple pretzels with your family sometime during Lent and share them at a meal. If your time is limited, frozen, ready-to-bake pretzels are available for microwaves or conventional ovens. As you eat the salty, hot pretzels together, you could talk a little about the Fatherland or read together about Germany and its people and customs. If your German relatives live nearby, you might invite them over to share the pretzels and stories. If there are German grandparents in your family, they will have stories of their own which will enrich your children's background immensely.

A long standing German custom for Holy Saturday is the lighting of fires on hill sides. When the fire is burning well, people gather around it to sing Easter hymns. Unless you live in an apartment with a communal yard space, it should not be too difficult to light a bonfire somewhere in your own back yard, fire codes permitting. Perhaps you can take the family for a walk in the woods some clear weekend during Lent to gather sticks for firewood. These can be saved and added to brush and other garden trash that you cleared last fall to make a respectable pile for a bonfire. On Holy Saturday, sometime after dark, trek the family out to your bonfire and light it. While the flames shoot upward hold hands and say a prayer, perhaps sing a song or two if your family likes to sing together. Even a small fire in an outdoor grill will do.

German children also enjoy rolling hard boiled eggs. They make tracks out of sticks for these. You may want to try a game that German children play with blown out eggs. A hollow decorated egg is placed in the center of a flat, clean table. Everyone gathers around. One person starts the game off by blowing the egg across the table. Whoever is closest to the egg blows it back across. No one may touch the egg, and anyone who lets the egg fall off the table has to leave the game. The last person remaining wins. This is a game best played with older children, I think. Very young ones tend to feel stranded if they have to leave a game at any time.

The Easter egg tree has its origins in Germany. This is an easy tradition to adopt and, after several years, all the props are there if you have been careful to save the eggs from season to season. Look around outside for a sturdy branch from a bush to serve as a miniature tree. I push mine into a coffee can filled with sand, then hide the can inside a pretty pottery crock. This goes on the dining room table and the sand is always kept moist. The eggs for this tree need to be blown out, then dyed and hung on the tree with thread. To hang the eggs, break a toothpick in half, tie some thread around the middle of one of the broken ends and then insert that end into the opening of the egg. The thread will then be secured for you to tie its other end to the branches of the Easter tree.

Easter in France

Fat Tuesday comes from the French words, *Mardi Gras*. Many years ago when people knew a long forty day fast lay ahead, they chose the day before Lent to feast and make merry. Carnivals were held and people frolicked, dressed in masks and costumes. Although we associate Mardi Gras with the French, such carnivals were and still are celebrated in many parts of Europe, not only for one day but the entire week proceeding Lent.

Unless you are from the beautiful city of New Orleans, you probably do not get caught up in Mardi Gras. If you want to celebrate your French ancestry, invite some friends and relatives for a party on the Tuesday before Lent begins. Simplify the preparations by making it a covered dish dinner, perhaps asking each family to bring an ethnic dish. Celebrate each other and gather strength for the long fast ahead. If you have the ambition (and the right kind of guests) ask everyone to wear a mask or even a costume. Religious observances needn't be grave and solemn.

Celebrating Fat Tuesday with only your immediate family can be just as rewarding. Remember that celebrations call for extra work, so start well ahead of time. If you are planning on having costumes or special ethnic foods, include the family in the planning *and* the work. Cook ahead of time and use the freezer to keep things fresh. Use the children to tend to details such as table setting, decorations, etc. As you involved your partner or spouse and your children in planning family prayers and Scripture reading, involve them now in every aspect of the celebration of this special feast.

Easter in Russia

In the Russia of the czars, Easter was the most important holiday of the year. Deeply rooted in the Slavic past, it is a tradition older than their written history. Today Russian people around the world share the beautiful rituals associated with Easter.

Celebrate *Maslenitsa* (Butter Festival) on the day before Lent begins. In pre-revolutionary Russia this was a week long festival with carnivals, masks and costumes reminiscent of the French Mardi Gras.

If your ethnic roots are Russian, the heart of your pre-Lenten celebration of Maslenitsa will be *bliny*. The bliny is a thin yeast pancake. The toppings distinguish this simple pancake and make it a festival cake. Hot from the pan, richly buttered, bliny are topped with caviar, sour cream, sliced salmon, smoked sturgeon, mushrooms, onions or pickled herring. Certainly, you will want to include toppings which your family may favor, such as strawberries, fruit jams, cream cheese or whatever scores high with them as a pancake topping.

Again, as with most other ethnic celebrations, the family gathering is important to this feast. Friends and relatives gathered around a table spread with bliny and toppings celebrate this charming feast in the Russian tradition as a preparation for Lenten fasting.

Easter eggs are very important to the Russian traditional

celebration. The intricately decorated Ukrainian eggs are beginning to enjoy a popularity in the United States as well. Schools and social groups often sponsor lessons in this ancient art.

Two years ago I decided it was time for all of us to be introduced to this special preparation for the Easter holiday. Feeling like a novice, I bought a decorating kit at an art supply store, and we went to work. It was fun, difficult, frustrating, and immensely rewarding. It was gratifying to watch my children doing something so timeless, something their ancestors had done for so many years.

If you decide to try the Ukrainian eggs, blow out the insides, rather than decorate a raw egg. My mother, an expert in this art, tells me that the raw insides will eventually dry out, but I have never been brave enough to put my completed colored eggs to this test. She has also suggested using large goose eggs for a really striking effect.

Surprisingly enough, even the younger children enjoy dying these intricate eggs, although the process is lengthy and the beginner's results are somewhat crude. It is from the doing, the comraderie, the laughter and the talk that enjoyment comes rather than from a perfectly finished product.

Two special foods are essential to the Russian celebration of Easter: *kulich* or Easter cake and *paskha*, a combination of cottage cheese, cream, eggs, raisins, almonds and candied fruit shaped somewhat like a pyramid.

In Russian communities, the kulich and some of the dyed eggs are taken to church to be blessed on Holy Saturday. Along with the paskha they become part of the special meal Russians will eat after the Easter Eve midnight service.

No one in our house is much good at staying up to celebrate anything after midnight. We have our big Easter feast on Easter day between noon and one o'clock. The table holds only Russian dishes, with the kulich, paskha and colored eggs prominently displayed.

One of the ethnic Easter traditions that our family delights in is egg battles. Colored hard boiled eggs are used for this. Each person chooses an egg and squares off against somebody else's egg. The challenger taps the opponent's egg lightly with the tip of his "champion." Whoever comes out uncracked is the new champ and goes on to challenge someone else. This continual egg "battle" goes on for days, with much joking and laughing and, one year, hot indignation when someone discovered that his "champ" had been mistakenly used in an egg sandwich.

Easter in Poland

In Poland, as in much of Europe, Lent begins with a carnival and party on Shrove Tuesday. On Good Friday the Poles have a custom of covering their mirrors in black veils to signify mourning. People looking into these veiled mirrors see their faces through a black shadow.

Holy Saturday is the day many Poles take their food baskets to church to be blessed. These baskets are covered with beautifully embroidered napkins. If you are good with a needle, you might want to make a special napkin for the Easter food basket. This can be a summer project, easily carried to poolside, or a winter project for those long evenings in front of the fire. Something special and beautiful like this can be a treasured piece to hand down to grown children. It keeps the ethnic traditions alive and grows in meaning as it comes down through the generations.

Another Polish tradition that is easily adopted and can be quite significant to the family is part of the Holy Saturday ritual of confession. The parents in the family ask each other's pardon for any unkind acts done against one another during the year. It might be meaningful to involve the children in this as well. During a quiet time set aside on Holy Saturday, take a little time to consciously put aside any malice you may be harboring against another and to ask that person's pardon. With most young children there is usually some kind of minor feud brewing, and this custom evolves into a nice lesson on reconciliation.

Pisanki are intricately dyed eggs, much like those of Russia. Pisanki decorate the Polish Easter table, along with flowers (artificial or real) and a beautiful, very intricately embroidered table cloth, used only for very special occasions.

One of the traditional main dishes for breaking the Easter fast is pork. In the old days this sometimes took the form of a stuffed pig's head. Polish sausage (Kielbasa), Poland's most famous and certainly most favored food, is part of this meal, along with Polish rye bread. At Easter breakfast the head of the house cuts up a colored egg and everyone at the table gets a piece. They exchange the greeting, "We wish you a happy alleluia."

Easter in Italy

On Holy Saturday, in the afternoon, Italians carry food to the churches to be blessed. Among the colored eggs and other foods in their baskets are sweet breads shaped in the forms of animals and dolls. Some Italians break the Easter fast in the afternoon of this day.

After dark on Holy Saturday, crosses are carried through town to a main crucifix which would be standing on the edge of fields or up in the mountains. You can visit a cross on Holy Saturday in the Italian tradition. If there is a crucifix in the house, set aside some time on Holy Saturday evening to gather the family around it for Scripture reading or prayer. Visit the crucifix at church if you like. Sometimes, inside a hushed and empty church, you can experience a quiet closeness to God that is very different from the communal celebration we are used to on Sundays.

Easter is a day for wearing best clothes and gathering the family for a celebration meal. The Monday after Easter is for friends, as well as family. On that day the Italians indulge in *La Scampagnata*, an annual all day picnic with baskets of food shared out in the green springtime fields and woods.

Christmas

How often have you watched Christmas fly into the new year and wished you had done something, *anything*, to bring a different tone to your holiday? Celebrating the Lord's birth with ethnic traditions will not take away the secular "gimmies" that young children are prone to, but it will add a dimension to your holiday that enriches your celebrations and deepens your family's roots in the soil of home.

England
So many of our American Christmas customs come from the English. Charles Dickens seems to have set the standard for decking the halls and making merry with an annual array of Christmas foods and customs.

The Yule log, which the Britons adopted from the Persians, was first called a *yole* log. In early Persia, once a year a tree was cut down and a section was cut from the trunk. The large, round section was marked off into four segments to represent the four seasons of the year. This crude calendar was called a yole and the log from which it came was called the yole log. As the seasons came around, the great calendar log was turned. A huge fire was kindled and the yole log was thrown into it as the people prayed for good fortune in the coming season. The yole log gradually became the Yule log and much later became a part of the Briton's Christmas celebration.

Some families cut off the dry end of their Christmas tree before discarding them. They put this piece away for a year until next Christmas. When the fireplace is going nicely, they throw the log in and gather around to read the Christmas story. The ancient barons and lords of England had huge fireplaces. It took many men to drag the Yule log from the woods into the great hall. By their standards the small trunk of a Christmas tree would hardly do, but it serves the modern family well.

In the 1400s King Henry VII introduced the wassail bowl to his subjects. The original contents of the wassail bowl may be a little strong for family sipping, as the bowl contained a mixture of toasted apples, spices and hot ale. If you have a pretty punch bowl, you could substitute hot cider or apple juice, spiced with cinnamon and cloves. Float some apples on top and sip this as you decorate the tree together.

Deep rooted in early English history is the singing of the carols. This goes back to the time when medieval minstrels went around from castle to castle singing for their food and lodging. Caroling with your family around the piano or walking from house to house in the snow (or fog or rain) can be a yearly tradition taken from your English forebears.

A tradition unique to the English is Boxing Day on December 26th. This day is devoted to visiting friends and tipping the various people who have served the family throughout the year, the milk maid, the postman, the paper carrier, etc. This custom began long ago when people dropped coins into various boxes set out for this purpose. The contents were distributed to the poor.

Roast goose, plum pudding and mince pie are three ethnic dishes that English families may want to serve at Christmas time. Plum pudding is traditionally made the first Sunday of Advent, called "Stir up" Sunday, and put away to season.

Deck your halls with greenery in the English manner. The Kissing Bough, coming from the Middles Ages, is easy to make. Laurel, ivy and rosemary are also used in English homes for decoration.

Germany

In Germany *lichtwochen* (light weeks) heralds the beginning of Advent. The people string colored lights and begin preparing for Christmas in earnest.

The Advent wreath is a German tradition that became popular as an Advent symbol all over the world. When your family gets out the Advent wreath, talk about its German origins. So too, the Christmas tree, now found in almost every Christian home in late December, originated in Germany. As you decorate your *Christbaum*, tell the children how the first Christmas tree was decorated with apples and how the candles were added in the sixteenth century. Sing the old German carol, "O Tannenbaum" while you trim the tree.

If you have time, bring home some books on Christmas customs from the library and learn about your ethnic traditions along with the children.

Gingerbread houses also come to us from Germany. In the United States, these beautiful candy structures can be purchased in a kit. Everything you need is there, including directions. I cannot think of anything we have done at Christmas time which has enchanted our children more than putting together the candy houses, with frosting everywhere, candy, nuts, and everyone helping with the gargantuan clean-up.

You can buy an Advent calendar and have the children take turns opening a window each day. The Advent calendar is popular in Germany and some very elaborate imported ones are available in the better stationery stores in the United States.

On December 6th St. Nicholas comes to visit each household in Germany to leave apples, nuts and sweets for all good children. The children hang their stockings over the foot of their beds or near the fireplaces for the saint to fill.

In the German tradition gifts are opened on Christmas Eve. Dressed in their best clothes, the family gathers for a supper which includes carp or a similar fish, potato dumplings, roast goose and red cabbage. As the meal ends, a variety of decorated cookies and cakes are brought to the table. Then the children wait in another room while the adults light the Christmas tree and put out the gifts. These gifts are not credited to Saint Nicholas, who has already made his visit in early December. In some households the Christ Child is the gift-bearer; in others, *Weihnachtamann* (Christmas Man) is the secular benefactor.

France
If your background is French, your children may want to put their shoes out by the fireplace on Christmas Eve instead of hanging stockings. *Le pere Noel* (Father Christmas) will fill them with toys or place them on top of the gifts he leaves. Le pere Noel is supposed to come on December 6th as he does in Germany, but in some French households he waits until Christmas Eve.

Christmas Eve dinner is called *Reveillon* which means "wake-up." Usually this meal is served after Midnight Mass on Christmas Eve, but there is no reason why you cannot serve it early in the day for convenience. It is a bountiful meal including roast goose, and concluding with the traditional French dessert cake, *Buche de Noel* or "Christmas Log."

Bringing in the Yule log (*trefoire*) is somewhat different in the French tradition. The log is brought in, placed inside the fireplace, and then the father of the house pours a glass of wine over it as a blessing.

Italy

In 1223 Saint Francis of Assisi introduced the *presepio*, or Nativity scene, to Italy. The first Nativity scenes required live people and animals. The Italian custom of the presepio spread all over Europe and the Americas.

Unique to the Italian culture is the *ceppo*, a pyramid-like structure. A ceppo is difficult to find unless you travel in Italy or come upon one at a flea market or auction. Italians use the ceppo for displaying Christmas ornaments. The broad lowest shelf is often reserved for the presepio.

For the Italian Christmas Eve dinner seven fish dishes are put on the table. These can be as complicated as calamare (squid) in sauce or as simple as a dish of sardines. No meat is allowed at this meal, and dessert is the traditional *panettone*, a raisin and candied fruit studded yeast cake.

On Christmas day children write letters to their parents asking their forgiveness for any unkindness or disobedience during the year. They hide these letters under the father's plate and when he "finds" them during Christmas day dinner, he reads them aloud at the table.

Le Befana is a kindly, old woman who comes down the chimney much like Santa Clause with gifts for the children. This is a difficult tradition to transplant because La Befana makes her visit on January 6th. I could never convince our children to wait that long for gifts when everyone else is being gifted on Christmas day.

Poland

For the family-centered Poles, Christmas is more a time for gathering the clan together, making ornaments and telling stories than for elaborate gift-giving.

On December 6th Saint Nicholas comes with gifts for the children. I have often though how nice it would be to get this gift-giving over with early, allowing time to concentrate on creating a more spiritual atmosphere for the remainder of the Christmas season. Unfortunately, with at least one Santa believer constantly present in the house, I have never been brave enough to buck the tide of Santa's Christmas Eve arrival. Maybe next year.

Christmas Eve day is a day of fasting. With the appearance of the first evening star the *wigilia* or Christmas Eve dinner officially begins. The table is set with a decorated cloth and the plates turned upside down. There is an extra setting, complete with silverware, napkin and china. This is for the unexpected guest. The Poles believe that it is important to welcome any stranger into their homes on this special night. Somewhere on the table should be some straw to remind the family that Jesus was born in humility in a stable. As each child upturns his plate, he finds a coin hidden beneath it, a gift from his parents.

There must be an odd number of foods for luck and each must be tasted by everyone at the table. Unique to the Polish tradition is the *oplatek* or wafer that is shared by the family. These wafers might be found in the ethnic Polish communities of such large cities as Chicago. The oplatek is stamped with nativity scenes and resembles the communion wafer used in the Catholic Mass. The parents break off a piece of the oplatek and dip it in honey, and then eat it. The rest is shared with everyone at the table. The father pronounces a benediction over the wafer about unity and staying close to home and family. So important is this symbol of unity to the Poles that they often send pieces of the oplatek to distant family in Christmas cards.

Christmas is a quiet day spent with the family. No one does any work, not even cooking. All the foods have been prepared the day before and are simply heated. A traditional Polish Christmas does not end with Christmas day, but lasts until Epiphany, the feast of the three kings.

Making the Ethnic Connection

As with any alteration you bring to the pattern of family life, go slowly in introducing ethnic celebrations of holidays. Some of these traditions require very little extra time and work, while others require an appreciable amount of both. Some, like the Polish custom of receiving gifts on December 6th, require a complete alteration of established patterns.

You and your spouse or partner need to be in accord before any of these traditions can be successfully introduced. If your holidays have been more secular than spiritual, a lot of groundwork needs to be laid before there can be a major change in your style of celebration.

As a single parent, you may want to join with another adult for many of these ethnic traditions. Some of them can be quietly celebrated with just your immediate family, but many need the participation of friends or relatives to bring about their complete fulfillment.

Follow the same rules here as you followed in introducing Scripture reading, family prayer and family liturgies to your family: talk with your spouse or partner; talk with your older children; prepare yourself as much as needed; go slowly at first. Do not take on too much the first year. Holiday traditions have a way of taking root, and before you have turned around you may find yourself stuck with a lot of time-consuming customs that you do not really want.

Feel free to add holiday traditions from ethnic groups other than your own. Each country has so many beautiful and spiritual customs, and many are easily adaptable. We have the Christmas tree from Germany, the creche from Italy and Shrove Tuesday from England.

Grandparents can be a wonderful source of ethnic enrichment for your family. If they have not actually lived the Old World traditions, most likely their parents have. If you are lucky enough to have family living in Europe write to them and ask them to explain their holiday rituals and traditions.

Setting aside some table linen or china to be used only for the great feasts of the year is a way of lending importance and continuity to these special days. Most important of all is the joy you bring to these celebrations. It does no good to wear yourself out with preparations, only to find your nerves worn so thin by the time the holiday comes that you cannot enjoy anything or anyone. Never forego the joy for the trappings.

The spirituality, family unity and gaiety of these ethnic holiday celebrations have been with us for hundreds of years. Let us hope they will continue to enrich our lives for many more.

Appendices

The Light of the World—An Irish Christmas Custom

Mary Dalton, Director of Religious Education
Our Sunday Visitor, Huntington, Indiana

One of the most abiding and popular Irish Christmas customs is the lighting of candles to celebrate the coming of Christ. My parents practiced this custom in their native homeland and continued to share it with their own family after coming to the United States. For the Irish, the season of Advent was a time of austerity. To prepare for the joy of Christmas, the Irish entered into a spiritual retreat lasting for the four weeks of Advent. As a child, I remember the practices of Advent being very similar to Lenten practices. Although, liturgically, the Church has always made a marked distinction between the period of waiting and preparation known as Advent and the period of penitence known as Lent, the lived experience of both of these seasons to a young child was markedly similar. Today, as the baptismal character of Lent has been recovered through the renewal of the Church's liturgy, we have begun to stress Lent as a time of preparation, preparation for a more vigorous commitment to our baptismal calling. Consequently, the two seasons of Advent and Lent continue to share a great deal in common.

All through Advent, our spiritual preparation was done as a family. My father gathered us together on the first Sunday of Advent and helped each of us determine the practice or practices which we would choose to actively prepare ourselves for Christmas. Great stress was always placed on the fact that our Advent practices should be done not only to help ourselves become more worthy of the coming of Jesus, but also to bring more happiness into the lives of others.

The term "Incarnational Theology" was certainly never used in our household, but its meaning was implicit during Advent and during the celebration of light on Christmas Eve. We were encouraged to do kind acts for other family members as well as friends, and equally encouraged to go without some type of treat or entertainment during Advent while putting the money saved by this abstention aside to be given to the poor and needy. Abstaining from food or entertainment was never seen as an end in itself, but rather as a means to prepare ourselves spiritually for Christmas and to recognize Christ's Incarnation in His people. I recall this emphasis on Christ's Incarnational presence among all people as one of the strongest beliefs my parents shared with me while I was growing up. The custom of the lighting of the candles on Christmas Eve demonstrated this belief in a strong, visual manner.

On the night of Christmas Eve, the entire family would process around the house, placing a lighted candle in every window. My parents would tell us the stories of how, in Ireland, this practice was done so that Jesus might know that He was welcomed into their home when He came again on Christmas. This lovely symbol, reminding us that Jesus is the Light of the World and that we also are to be light to others, must have been particularly striking on the wind-swept Irish moors before electricity came to the rural areas of Ireland. With just the light from the hearth, and the candles in the window against the blackness of the long winter night, this was a powerful reminder that the Christian family was calling to Emmanuel to come and ransom us.

The symbol of the lighted candles had another purpose as well. Oftentimes strangers would become lost in the barren hills. The candles spoke to anyone who might be out there in the night that this was a Christian home and the stranger was welcome, because the stranger might indeed be the Christ. I always loved this part of the story. It seemed that my parents had so many tales to tell us of people they knew or knew of in their homeland who had befriended "strangers," only to have the strangers disappear! The "stranger" was always seen as a Christ-figure. Whether the stories I was told were true or not, I will probably never know, but they provided me with a deep conviction that Jesus appears to us in many guises, if we are only alert to His presence.

After lighting all of the candles, our family returned to the living room, where the youngest member placed the statue of the infant Jesus into the manger which had been set up but left empty at the beginning of Advent. At this point we all sang the verses to "O Come, O Come Emmanuel."

The custom of the lighting of the candles in the window is very much alive in many churches throughout the country. Churches have begun to encourage their people to place candles in sand bases, and put them in rows outside their homes to light the way for the Christ Child. One special Christmas Eve I drove with my mother around her neighborhood where this custom is widely practiced. It was very quiet, a layer of snow on the ground and on almost every block were these lovely candles in opaque milk containers or brown bags. The effect was profound. In an age when many people become discouraged at the commercialism of Christmas, here was evidence in house after house, block after block, of public witness to why we celebrate this beautiful feast of our transformation in Christ.

Catholic Cajun Experience

Sister Carmelita Latiolais, Director of Religious Education
Diocese of Lafayette, Lafayette, Louisiana

The Cajun people are Louisianians descended from French-speaking Acadians. Acadia is an earlier name for Nova Scotia. Out of the tribulations these people suffered in their early history—their land traded among the more powerful nations, their Catholic faith threatened, their families separated and its members exiled—has grown a rich core of religious expression.

Seeking religious freedom and greater opportunity, the Acadians settled in Louisiana. Here they found the French language and the Catholic faith already existing. Their descendants form the major part of the population of many small towns in Southwest Louisiana. In this part of the country, to be Cajun is to be Catholic. Even those who do not participate regularly consider the Catholic faith an important part of their lives, especially in rearing their children.

The difficult journey of their ancestors has formed a rugged yet warm and hospitable people. It is as though the struggles have generated a beautiful wisdom and *joi de vivre* (joy of life) in this unique group of people.

In families of Cajun descent, we often find great attention to family prayers, the rosary and other devotions. Religious art and symbols are prominently displayed (candles, large rosaries, palms, statues, etc.) in the home. Many families have a custom of praying the rosary or other prayers at family altars.

Unique religious customs are found in specific areas of Acadiana (Southwest Louisiana). In the small town of Catahoula, along the bayou, families have the custom of setting up a home altar for the veneration of the cross. On Good Friday morning, each family member spends time in prayer venerating the cross. Later in the morning, the entire family goes to a point about ten miles out of town to begin a traveling way of the cross led by the pastor. An interesting part of their tradition is that after the way of the cross, everyone goes back to their homes to eat pies that have been baked in preparation for this occasion. Good Friday thus became "pie day."

One of the first things a visitor to Acadiana notices is the cemeteries. The tombs are built above ground due to the high water level in the area. Culturally, cemeteries are very important to Cajun families. Weeks prior to All Saints Day, the cemeteries are full of families cleaning and white washing tombs. It is not unusual to see picnics in the cemeteries and find the people sharing stories of past times and people that have died. All Saints Day blessings are attended by large numbers of families. Often the rosary and other prayers accompany the blessing. Many pastors even celebrate Mass in the cemetery on this day. In the past, many families had their own cemeteries. One small town, in fact, has over thirty!

Individual families still pass on traditions of mourning. It is not unusual to seen Cajuns wearing dark clothes for months after a family death.

Closely related to the traditions surrounding death are the customs dealing with illness and healing. Many families pass on their own prayers for healing. Certain families have healers that are known as *traitures*. Cajuns will go to traitures for a wide variety of health problems, most often for the removal of warts. Traitures are not paid or even thanked because this healing is seen as a ministry.

Laissez le bon temps rouler (let the good times roll) is an expression often heard in Louisiana. Cajun people as a group are a people of great celebration. This sense of celebration is nurtured in the family and is part of the spirituality of the people. Individual families have their own traditions of celebrating as do parish and neighborhood communities. One such example is the yearly opening of the shrimp season in fishing communities. In the small town of Delcambre families gather to decorate their boats which join a parade on the canal. The shrimp festival officially begins with Mass followed by the blessing of the shrimp fleet. Either the local pastor or the bishop goes out to the shrimp boat accompanied by altar boys. He blesses the boats. This marks the beginning of the season.

The Cajun people have a rich tradition. The family unit and the Catholic faith are an integral part of this people's cultural expression and celebration.

Prayerful Polish Customs

Father Chester Wrzaszczak
St. Karol Private Chapel, Portland, Oregon

Two of the most popular family festivities among the people of Poland—and transported overseas—are as religious as they are joyful.

Winter Wonderland. The first is Christmas Eve.

With the Poles, Christmas Eve simultaneously ends the anticipatory Advent season and ushers in the Nativity holiday. It is deeply devotional. Fasting and abstinence, as during Lent, was Church law for many centuries for the four weeks preceding December 25. Hence, the final meal before Christmas feasting was a meatless one—but, oh, so divinely different!

A truly spiritual atmosphere permeated each Polish home as the hush of darkness ended a busy, bustling day. The head of the house, the father of the family (in those days), presided over a heavily laden table as the evening meal was the main meal and, therefore, a full meal, a special supper, featuring food not eaten together at any other time in the year.

We children were wide-eyed at the gaily decorated table cloth (only seen on big holy days) on which were set each one's dish upside down. Each plate rested on rustling, fragrant straw reminiscent, of course, of the straw in Bethlehem's manger. When the first course of fish or vegetable soup was to be served by Mother from a stack of bowls at her elbow, we were allowed to turn over our plates. Lo and behold! A freshly minted coin nestled in the center of the straw, a gift (before toys became popular) from our dear parents. One year, I recall clearly, before the Great Depression darkened our lives, each of us found a *gold* coin under our plates. My memory is vivid because this was the first time my hands held genuine gold. The glistening coin was a little larger than a dime, yet worth ten silver or paper dollars. I have never held a gold coin since—its use as currency is now illegal.

With the bowls steaming before our noses, our parents' present safely tucked away in our pockets, Dad led us in prayer. It was not the usual "Bless us, O Lord" but a longer, spontaneous yet traditional supplication.

The beginning of this prayer was a commemoration of the dead:

Heavenly Father, we left our loved ones in our motherland. Some we will never see again. They are with you. We pray we may all meet again one Christmas Day in the Bethlehem of heaven.

A petition followed:

Holy Family, Jesus, Mary and Joseph, keep our family in health, spiritual and physical, and rich in grace, if not in worldly goods.

Failure to live up to divine expectation also was included:

We're sorry we were not as holy as your Holy Family, Jesus, in this past year. We'll try harder in the New Year.

Finally, gratitude for the gift of Christmas:

We're humbly grateful for giving us this joyful season at a time of the year when the world is cold and dark. Direct any homeless orphan or weary traveler to our door on this Holy Night. . . .

At this, all eyes turned toward an empty chair before a fully set place at the table. It guaranteed the truth of our final petition. We were ready to welcome anyone not having a home or family to go to on Christmas Eve.

With almost a shouted "Amen" from us fidgeting and by now very hungry offspring, Father then, on this special occasion, performed perhaps his most meaningful role as head of the family. He reached for the long oval platter in front of him on which lay a green envelope, four by six inches with red lettering on top, possibly from the parish church, more often from relatives in Poland. It contained the famous Christmas wafer known as the *Oplatek* (ope-pwatt-tek). Dad prayed for what the wafer symbolized, family unity:

Almighty Lord, one God yet Three Persons, a Divine Unity, keep us always one in love, in one and the same faith and in your one holy, Catholic Church always.

Then, to show how we were to be united as a family, Dad took out from the envelope one wafer, oh so thin, so fragile, so white, so delicate. He turned to Mother with it. She broke off a fragment. Dad then broke off a morsel from her piece. They both dipped their portions in honey and swallowed the sweet servings with love in their eyes and a sweet smile on their lips. It looked like a non-liturgical but very solemn communion service. Dad then shared the rest of the oblong delicate bread with each of us, gravely pronouncing a brief benediction over us, such as "Let's all be one as God is one" or "Stay close to home and family." Thus, we shared with our caring and concerned parents a tremendous truth, now unfortunately regarded as a trite motto: The family that prays together, stays together.

When the last fragment was shared, there was, momentarily, disorder around the table. We kids got out of our chairs or reached over to grasp in wonder—and eat at random—the remaining sheets of the Oplatek. How we admired with oohs and aahs the different Nativity scenes stamped into each wafer-sheet: Jesus, Mary and Joseph surrounded by angels; the Holy Family amid the shepherds and their flocks; the Magi bringing gifts, a dozen or so such tableaus in all.

Returning to our places we were now served by Mother the first course, fish soup. Mother's soup was piping hot with flakes of white fish (trout, bass or cod), large chunks of potatoes (Polish soups invariably contain potatoes) and clusters of parsley. Sometimes it was sour cream soup with celery.

Soup was followed by two kinds of fish—cold herring with raw onion rings and beads of pepper as well as freshly baked salmon or pike. Deep bowls of sauerkraut with mushrooms, often picked in fall or purchased and left to hang and dry on the pantry door, were also served. The mushrooms were a savory substitute for the forbidden meat, usually pork.

No Polish meal would be complete without the national favorite, *pierogi* (pyeh-rug-ghee). These are really Polish blintzes (thin pancakes), sauteed in butter and filled with a Polish style, sweetened cottage cheese called *twarog* (tvah-rug). Other fillings included sauerkraut or prunes and, in prosperous years, cherries or berries. Rye bread, dark and light, with or without caraway seeds sown over a scrumptious, mouth-watering crust, completed the Vigil meal.

If the Christmas tree had not been put up early in the day (never before December 24), Dad would lead the family after supper in this exciting task. Again, he would offer a prayer, sometimes informally as he enthroned the tree in its stand.

May this tree brighten our home as it brightened the forest with its bright green amid the winter's gloom.

Younger children, however, were sent to bed because their eyelids were drooping and because the ornaments would not survive their inexperienced childish handling. Mom usually presided over their evening prayers, often kneeling on the hard wooden floor alongside them by the bed. They prayed, "Goodnight Jesus. We love you. You love us."

Spring Special. The second splendid family feast occurring among Poles, both in their native land as well as in exile or in voluntary diaspora in every part of the globe, was the Easter Morning Breakfast. True, every item and morsel of food in the traditional Easter baskets had been blessed by the priest in church the day before, yet Dad prayed briefly over the pungent aromatic contents, which would constitute our Paschal morning meal:

May this food, which reminds us of the new life of spring, bring us all to the eternal life won for us by the Lamb of God, who arose from the dead on this Easter Day.

The food to which Father alluded was indeed symbolic, a reminder of new life. Lining the Easter baskets were the traditional colored eggs. In the children's baskets the eggs were of candy as well. In the center, at the very bottom, one basket contained a lamb made of cake with wavy icing representing its wooly coat, a red collar and a red banner with a white cross on each, announcing the triumph of the "Lamb once slain who dies no more." A smaller but, oh so cute, second lamb, made of butter with pepper beads for eyes and the familiar red collar with its white cross lay in another basket. In still another, the heaviest and most nourishing of all, was the roast ham encircled by one of Poland's most famous and favorite foods, *Kielbasa* (kel-bah-sah), the staple of Polish diets. Atop the two meats was the means of holding them, hygienically, I always say, namely, Polish rye bread. It was not the usual long loaf but a special round one with a cross etched out by the baker on its surface. In a small jar, tightly closed, was the other ingredient for the bread and meat, freshly grated horseradish. (How we older children hated this most unpopular feature of Holy Saturday preparation—grating the stalks of horseradish. Sharp metallic tips on the hand grater not only shredded the radish but often skinned our knuckles. Ouch! We were reminded to offer this up to Jesus, Who suffered so on the cross for us the day before, Good Friday. It was indeed a penitential exercise.)

Other preparations for Easter Sunday on Holy Saturday included the cleaning of the whole house. While Dad was busy making the Polish sausage and Mom cooking the ham, we children mopped, dusted, beat the rugs, then, the fun part, colored Easter eggs.

Once the fragrant foods were prepared and evening drew on, our parents, too, had to "clean up," that is, spiritually, so as to celebrate the Paschal Mystery worthily the next day. They had their "Easter Duty" to perform as annual confession was then labelled. With Polish parents there was a traditional ritual necessary (within the privacy of the home) to be observed. Before setting out for church to seek absolution for their transgressions, it was customary for married couples to ask each other's pardon. By the time we were ten years of age, we became conscious of what was going on between our parents, and we enjoyed the yearly scenario that took place every Holy Saturday night at our house.

Mother, most likely, asked Dad to forgive her failings in the secrecy of their bedroom. Dad, however, always seemed to procrastinate in seeking her pardon. He just could not get the words out. So, he would begin edging toward the kitchen door (front door for guests only), inch by inch, eyeing the wall clock as its hands crawled toward seven o'clock, the start of confessions at Five Holy Martyrs Church, across the street from us. Finally, as we watched with bated breath, Dad, hand already on the door knob, would turn in Mother's direction (she sat patiently at the kitchen table, a cup of coffee before her), and with great difficulty ask in a meek and resigned tone of voice, not "I'm so, so-, sorry" or "I ap-, apologize" but indirectly, "Am, am I for-, forgiven?"

Silence. A momentary silence.

Then Mom would give Dad a rather reproachful look, wave her hands at him and hastily reply, "You're forgiven. Go on. I'll follow you later."

We all exhaled a deep sigh of relief.

Thus, the next morning our parents could lead us in prayer with peaceful, reconciled consciences.

For you fathers and mothers not having a rich, ethnic background so admirably adept for family prayer, do not despair. There is a plethora of American holidays and observances that can inspire family prayer as well as instruction for your children. Flag Day is terrific for explaining patriotism and respect for our symbol of freedom, followed by an appropriate home-made, spontaneous or prepared prayer. The church's calendar, too, offers ample opportunity for home devotions—St. Valentine's Day, the Parish Patron Saint day, St. Joseph, St. Patrick, St. Ludmilla (now there's a challenge!), your own namesdays, etc. are awaiting you.

Give these a try. You and your children will be better for it.

Celebration and Prayer in African-American Families

Nathan W. Jones, Ph.D.
Consultant, Archdiocese of Chicago

Even in the darkest hours, we have never failed to hold fast to one another. Our journey has confirmed our experience that faith is greater than fear. Our grandparents knew this and taught this lesson in their stories, songs, prayers, and most importantly, in their overwhelming strength. As our struggles continue, we must reclaim this strength—this faith— for our lives today.

Unity Circle. The best starting place for prayer is always our own family and circle of loving relationships. There is no such thing as a single ant or a solitary bee. Separated from the ant hill or the beehive, the individual insects die. This is true for us as well. When we lose one another and no longer feel comfortable with our roots, we become dangerously lost. One practice which fosters the qualities we acknowledge as essential for our households is making a Unity Circle.

Take the responsibility to call together everyone in your household for a Unity circle. It does not require a special occasion, simply the desire to strengthen the bond of unity and not lose touch with one another.

If there is some resistance by certain members of the household, gently encourage their participation. Make it clear that the Unity Circle is not an opportunity to release anger toward others but primarily an occasion to strengthen the quality of love.

In most cultures, circles symbolize the power of connectedness. Within the circle there is strength and unity. The evil that seeks to destroy us cannot penetrate our circle of love. Keeping the circle strong prevents the intrusion of divisive forces. Because we are Catholic-Christians we are aware that relationships are reflections of God's love for us. A Unity Circle is a kind of "sacrament," that is, we express outwardly what we feel inside.

Here's a suggested approach:

Getting Everyone's Attention. Turn off the television and radio. Call attention to the specialness of these moments. Assemble in a regular space such as the living room or dining area.

Atmosphere. Lighting a candle, dimming the lights, or playing soft music creates a prayerful environment of readiness.

Opening. As individuals join the circle, keep a few moments of silence in order for the inner and outer noise to quiet. Begin with a short Bible passage selected by a family member. Frequently the Sunday lectionary readings are an excellent source. At other times, begin by humming a familiar spiritual, hymn or popular song.

Testimonies. Invite family members to state how they are feeling inside (lousy, wary, enthused, angry, delighted). Do not insist that everyone speak. Invite persons to share a word about recent happenings in the household. Perhaps someone is praised for generosity, another is having a birthday, or a neighbor is ill. Bring all these concerns—positive and negative—to this Unity Circle.

Prayer. When the leader observes that everyone has been given the opportunity to speak, she/he invites someone moved by God's Spirit to lead the family in a word of prayer. The family might conclude the prayer with, "Amen."

Conclusion. Bringing the Unity Circle to conclusion is as simple as it began. Invite persons to give one another a round of applause by saying, "Now, let's give God, alive and well in our family, a round of applause!"

At other times, you might choose to conclude by embracing one another.

Lighting Festival Lights. African-Americans believe that it's not only *what* you do, but *how* you do it that is important. Therefore, take time on special occasions to light candles of love and hope.

In a comfortable space invite the children and other family members to assemble in a circle. We remember that circles express unity, a quality we seek to promote.

Four candles of any size, shape or color are attractively placed on a low table for everyone to see. The eldest member of the household reverently lights one candle at a time while the household recites the following affirmations:

Candle 1: We commit ourselves to work responsibly today. Everything else is jive (phony).

Candle 2: To study helps us find answers to our problems.

Candle 3: To create bridges out of our burdens is a lesson

from our elders.

Candle 4: To build together as a people is a sacred task.

Conclude with a music selection, a spontaneous prayer or a gesture of love.

Holding and Blessing. Parents and caregivers should be alert to special times when a child—or any family member—will benefit from the closeness of a warm hug. Here is one human gesture rich in reminders of God's love for us.

Just as there are occasions for correction and disciplining, we must never fail to "give a little sugar" and bring children close to us. Holding them in ways that convey "I accept you as you are" or "I want you to be the best you," balance other times when adults are unconsciously harsh and out of control.

Understanding the importance of prayer, celebration and unity allows us to appreciate the strengths we already possess. In a society where African-Americans are still not totally accepted nor appreciated, taking time to listen to one another, hold one another, light candles of hope, and invite God's visitation—these are occasions we never, ever outgrow.

Of course, there are celebrations that are traditional such as birthdays, retirement, graduations, anniversaries. And there are cultural and religious holidays such as Kwanzaa, Juneteenth Day, Dr. King's Birthday, and church seasons. However, these observances become weak if they are not reinforced by practices of prayer and unity in our families throughout the year.

Resources

Scripture Reading

The Concise Catholic Dictionary for Parents and Religion Teachers
Reynolds R. and Rosemary Ekstrom
Twenty-third Publications
P.O. Box 180
Mystic, CT 06355

The Family and the Bible
Mary Reed Newland (out of print)

Alone With God: A Manual of Biblical Meditation
Campbell McAlpine
Bethany House
6820 Auto Club Road
Minneapolis, MN 55438

The One Year Bible
Tyndale House Publishers
336 Gundersen Drive
P.O. Box 80
Wheaton, IL 60189

Daily Light: New King James Version Daily Meditations, Special Devotions for Special Occasions
Thomas Nelson Publishers
P.O. Box 141000
Nelson Pl. at Elm Hill Pike
Nashville, TN 37214

The One Year Book of Family Devotions
Tyndale House Publishers
(see above)

How to Read the Bible Every Day
Carmen Rojas
Servant Books
840 Airport Boulevard
Ann Arbor, MI 48107

Bible Tapes

The Living Bible
Tyndale House Publishers
(see above)

King James Version, Holy Bible
Economy Bible Cassettes
P.O. Box 5767
Arlington, Texas 76005

New International Version
Praise, Psalms and Proverbs
Hosanna Music
Ebscosound, Inc.
El Toro, CA

Family Prayers

How to Pray for Your Children
Quin Sherrer
Aglow Publications
P.O. Box 1548
Lynwood, WA 98046-1558

Mel Bay's Family Worship Handbook
William Bay
Mel Bay Productions, Inc.
#4 Industrial Drive
Pacific, MO 63069-0066

Praying God's Word
Ed Dufresne
Harrison House, Inc.
P.O. Box 35035
Tulsa, OK 74153

When God Is At Home With Your Family
David M. Thomas
Abbey Press
Highway 545
St. Meinrad, IN 47577
Guidelines for Family Worship
Anna Lee Carlton
Warner Press
1200 East Fifth Street
Anderson, IN 46012
Prayers for the Domestic Church
Edward Hays
Forest of Peace Books, Inc.
Route One, Box 247
Easton, KS 66020
Praying the Daily Gospels
Philip St. Romain
Ave Maria Press
Notre Dame, IN 46556
Sunday Throughout the Week
Gaynell Cronin
Ave Maria Press
(see above)

Family Celebrations

The Blessing Cup
Rock Travnikar, OFM
St. Anthony Messenger Press
1615 Republic Street
Cincinnati, OH 45210
Saints, Signs and Symbols
W. Ellwood Post
Morehouse, Barlaw Co.
78 Danbury Road
Wilton, CT 06897
Jewish Family Celebrations
Arlene Rossen Cardozo
St. Martin's Press
175 Fifth Avenue
New York, NY 10010
Children of the Church

Servants of the Immaculate
Heart of Mary
Monroe, MI
(out of print)
The Way
Josemaria Escriva de Balaguer
Scepter Publishers
481 Main Street
New Rochelle, NY 10801
All About Jewish Holidays and Customs
Morris Epstein
Ktav Publishing House, Inc.
Box 6249
Hoboken, NJ 07030
Religious Customs in the Family
Francis Weiser, S.J.
Liturgical Press
St. John's Abbey
Collegeville, MN 56312
A Book of Feasts and Seasons
Joanna Bogle
(out of print)
The Family Lenten Handbook: Change My Heart
Jean Marie Hiesberger, Gen. ed.
Paulist Press
997 MacArthur Boulevard
Mahwah, NJ 07430
Blessings For God's People
Reverend Thomas G. Simons
Ave Maria Press
(see above)